HUMAN TRAFFIC

HUMAN TRAFFIC

Sex, Slaves and Immigration

Craig McGill

First published in Great Britain in 2003 by Vision Paperbacks,
a division of Satin Publications Ltd.
101 Southwark Street
London SE1 0JF
UK
info@visionpaperbacks.co.uk
www.visionpaperbacks.co.uk
Publisher: Sheena Dewan

A catalogue record for this book
is available from the British Library.

ISBN: 1-904132-17-0

2 4 6 8 10 9 7 5 3

Cover photograph: American Science and
Engineering, Inc., Billerica, Massachusetts, USA
Cover design by Button One-to-One

Typeset by M Rules
Printed and bound in the UK by Mackays of Chatham Ltd,
Chatham, Kent

CONTENTS

Contents

ACKNOWLEDGEMENTS

The acknowledgements for this book could fill another book on their own, but many people have requested anonymity – or even in some cases were unaware they were speaking to a reporter – and as such it would be unfair to put anyone at risk by singling them out for praise, so I will instead just thank everyone who helped me in this book. It may be my name on the cover but more than 100 people from across the globe played a part in this book being written.

However, some people who certainly deserve praise and thanks include the team at Vision for encouraging this book, financing it and being understanding when deadlines were being pushed back as I tried to find the proper tone and balance for the book. So heartfelt gratitude has to go to everyone there, including Charlotte Cole, Emily Bird, Sheena Dewan and Stella Wood.

Thanks also has to go to Michael Tierney for at times brutal words of honesty and encouragement. It would also be remiss not to thank Mike Graham and his team at the *Scottish Daily Mirror*, including Shaun Milne, Ron Moore and Dawn Chantry, for enabling me to work on this book while remaining there as a worker.

Lastly, thanks for the incredible cover image goes to American Science & Engineering, Inc., Dr Joseph Callerame and Laura Berman as well as Jackson Bain of Bain and Associates, Inc., for their help in acquiring the image.

Others who deserve some thanks for their help include Stephen Turner, Ian Gould, Kristen Conte and Kazumoto Ohno.

INTRODUCTION

- More than 20 million people are on the move every year – of these, only around 2 million go to America, 250,000 to the UK, and 150,000 leave the UK. Over half of these are doing so with no guarantee they will be accepted in their new country, as they are travelling illegally.
- At least 2,500 people die every year while attempting to reach a new homeland. Causes of death include: drowning at sea, being killed by the authorities, being left to die by smugglers, being trapped in a cargo container or freezing to death in the undercarriage of a plane.
- The illegal immigration industry is a financial area worth more than US$10 billion a year – and is expected to rise over the coming years. Depending on the journey taken, a person can pay anything from US$5,000 to more than US$50,000. It is a growth industry for criminals, especially considering that courts, compared to drugs and arms smuggling, do not hand out harsh penalties for people smuggling.

While some people may contest the figures and definitions used in this book, I have used those that are, perhaps, least contentious – one problem is that very few countries seem to be able to agree on what defines an immigrant.

There is no simple reason why people decide to leave their home country. Some do so because they have fallen in love with someone they want to be with. Some flee because they are being tortured for their political or religious beliefs (these are dictionary-definition refugees – those avoiding persecution). Others move away to find work and more money, so that they can provide for their families back home (ie economic migrants). More disturbingly, others move so they can work for gangsters or earn a living shuttling drugs between two countries, while others still find themselves kidnapped to exist as sex slaves.

The matter becomes more complex when you consider that many people who become legal citizens of a country after meeting certain criteria (sometimes financial, sometimes not) often use illegal means to get there. In addition, studies have shown that smuggled immigrants not only form part of every country's black economy, but they can also be useful to the real economy. Very often they are doing the jobs that no one else will do, helping their adopted country to run 'business as usual'.

Helping these people move from one country to another is an illegal yet growing industry in human traffic. In most cases, people are smuggled from east (Asia, Russia) and south (Mexico, Africa) to west (Europe, USA) and north (USA, Canada).

Migrants from Asia's main route is via the southern ex-USSR countries (including Kazakhstan, Kyrgyzstan, Uzbekistan, Tajikistan and Turkmenistan), to Russia and from there via the Ukraine, Slovakia and the Czech Republic to Western European countries, or even further on to the United States and Canada. There is also the 'classical Balkan route', which carries people from Asia via Iran and Turkey and the Balkan states to Western Europe.

Africa too is experiencing mass migration to Europe. Particularly during summer months, Spain and Germany face the arrival of thousands of illegal immigrants originating from the Sub-Saharan region of the African continent. These people travel from Morocco to Southern Spain by using the narrow Strait of Gibraltar where only 21 kilometres separate Europe and Africa.

South Africa is unusual within Africa in being a destination country, for mostly Asian migrants – particularly Chinese nationals. Much of this migration seems to be connected to South-East Asian smuggling networks. A large number of Chinese nationals are travelling to South Africa with fraudulent documents or making 'questionable' journeys to contact countries such as Swaziland, Lesotho or Mozambique. From South Africa, willing migrants may often continue their journey to the USA but also to European countries by plane.

As has been well reported, Australia is also facing a growing number of illegal immigrants. They come mostly from the Middle East and South Asia, landing on Australia's western coasts and especially on Christmas Island, which is located relatively close to the Indonesian archipelago. Refugees first enter Malaysia, where they are taken to the south before making a short ferry crossing to the Indonesian island of Batam. From there it is not difficult to reach Jakarta and go on to the southern Indonesian islands of Bali, Flores or Lombok, where they embark for Australia. Very often, however, they meet a hostile police and immigration force before they find land.

Smuggling networks in the USA focus more and more on Central and South America, where they maintain the links to Mexican people smugglers necessary to move illegal migrants via Mexico to North America.

I wanted to find out who are the real people behind the media stories. Why do people risk everything to build a new life halfway across the world? What do they find when they get there? Who helps them to travel? And when and why do things go wrong? What is the law enforcement agencies' perspective? Are they looking out for people's safety or just interested in quotas?

The words of people who have been involved in immigration are far more powerful and informative than anything I could write and, as such, this book mostly allows these people to speak for themselves. Some of them were reluctant to speak; some did not know their words would end up in a book; others spoke freely, determined to prevent others suffering the way they have. We hear from legal and illegal immigrants, the smugglers and the smuggled, politicians, police and other enforcement agencies worldwide. Surprisingly, perhaps, some of the nicest people I met while researching *Human Traffic* were the criminals, who saw themselves as businessmen providing a service. And some of the least pleasant were supposedly on the side of law and order. But there is good and bad on every side – only by listening to everyone involved in a situation can you try to understand it, and that is what I attempt to do with this book. By building up an inclusive (but by no means exhaustive) picture I have tried to identify just what the 'problem' of immigration really might be.

PART 1
THE IMMIGRANTS

1

FROM RICE FIELDS TO GOLDEN MOUNTAINS: ESCAPING CHINA

Xie Li likes America. 'It is the land of the free,' he says, standing in the heart of San Francisco's Chinatown, 'but it is not free to get here – anything but.'

Xie is like the millions of others who over the years have been smuggled into the USA and Europe and are now working away, building new lives for themselves.

Asia is the hotbed of immigration. More people leave to go elsewhere – normally the USA, Britain, Japan or Australia – than from anywhere else. Japan is the only country in Asia to have the problem of people being smuggled into the country; everyone else is concerned with people leaving.

One of the biggest problem areas is the Fujian province on China's south-east coast. There emigrating is almost a way of life, with 10 million Fujianese living abroad. Ironically, parts of Fujian have a better rate of living than elsewhere in the country. For example, in Fuzhou, incomes are high because of cheap clothing sent out for export around the world. But if life is tolerable here, why would anyone want to move? A walk around Fuzhou's cramped winding streets quickly gives you an answer.

All along Fujian's coast, smart new private houses are being built, some the size of small mansions, all with money sent back by relations in the West. And in a country where space is a premium, there is nothing better. That and more money. Those who leave home today are doing so for the same reason as millions over the years – a better life and more money.

The average Chinese villager can make around US$50–75 a month, whereas in America they can make approximately US$1,500 per month. And that's not in a skilled job, but in what many would consider a menial task with no language or work skills. Chinese have been attracted by this better life for almost 200 years.

In 1820 the first Chinese immigrants to arrive at San Francisco in the United States came from the Fujian province. San Francisco was also the area that suffered the most in the anti-Chinese riots of 1880, which led to the Chinese Exclusion Act of 1882, barring unskilled Chinese labourers from the USA.

But then, as now, laws did not deter people from moving on to find a better life for themselves. It's now a lot harder, but if you are willing to break the law and pay a lot of money it can still be done.

Chinese Triad gangs – and the others in the business – make an estimated US$6 billion per year smuggling more than 100,000 Chinese aliens into the USA. The industry started to pick up considerably in the 1980s, when farmers in Fujian lost their land to factories, which hired mostly young women. Networks – dubbed by some 'bamboo networks' – soon developed to smuggle people to Taiwan, South-East Asia, Canada and Mexico.

The smuggling routes follow along well-established routes that have been used for years to carry goods and smuggle drugs. Countries like Belize, Jamaica, the Dominican Republic, Paraguay, Mexico and Russia have all been involved at some point.

Many Chinese trade their passport for a Taiwanese passport, and are then moved to a country such as the Dominican Republic, for continuing passage to the United States. China's Public Security Bureau estimates that there are half a million Chinese waiting for transit to the West in Moscow, Ho Chi Minh City, Bangkok, Africa, Brazil, Mexico, Romania and Bulgaria. Final destinations include the USA, the UK, Australia, Austria, Italy, Germany and the Czech Republic, but America by far is the dreamland for many of them, with most ending up in San Francisco or New York.

Xie Li eventually decided that he wanted to go to America. He worked in a factory but, like many his age, born in the early 1970s, he had a hunger to go elsewhere. He saw the homes being built and the tales of how good it was elsewhere in the world. He also knew it wouldn't be cheap.

'I didn't know where I wanted to go, I just knew that I wanted to be doing as well as others and having the adventures they were having. It all sounded exciting, especially in America where people were earning what could take more than ten years to raise here in just one year.'

Along with some friends, he saved for a long time and his parents – who actively encouraged him to go – also saved, as they knew he would send money back when he could. According to Chinese-American scholar Ko-lin Chin, parents are very often the people who make their children go abroad: 'If you don't have a member living in the United States, it's a disgrace to your family; your family has no future; your family has nothing to say in the village; your family has no status.'

After years of saving, when he turned 28 Xie Li decided his time had come. He still did not have enough money, but the gang boss who he had contacted made him a few offers to help reduce the cost.

'I was offered a number of deals, ranging from flying to where I wanted to go with a fake passport to being smuggled in a container or even taking a very long route across land. The only deciding factor was what I could afford.

'My family and I had raised almost US$10,000, which the gang took as a down payment. I was told that, if I was captured or anything happened, that money would not come back to me.'

The next decision for Xie was where to go. He was lucky in that he had family in both Britain and America. They all agreed that if he came over, he could work for them in order to pay off his soon-to-be-arranged debt and they would also help out if they could, so he did not have to spend too many years paying back his 'loan'.

With that knowledge, Xie opted for being smuggled by cargo ship, which was affordable at US$25,000, as compared to the US$50,000 being charged for flight into a country with a passport and visa.

The snakeheads who were arranging for Xie's move left him in no uncertain terms that he would be visited weekly to collect money to keep paying back his debt. He also had the option of working for them when he was not working for his family.

Xie was also given another option. 'I was told that if I wanted, I could go to America and then have an organ removed, which they said would clear my debt instantly and also give me some money to start my new life with. If I sold a kidney, I would get US$15,000 – as well as being flown into America with a passport – and the prices went up from there.

'The snakeheads also let it be known that if I knew of anyone who would donate organs or if I could find healthy organs, then they would pay almost as good money for them, but that an organ in a live body was best. It was an incredible thought. They told me that it was one of the growth areas. People would put themselves forward to give an organ and in return would be flown in style to America – it seemed to be the only place for the organs to be taken to – with a false passport. They would then be taken to a place for the organ to be removed. Once they had recovered, they were free to go on their way and lead their lives with some new money. The organs would then be sold on for hundreds of thousands of dollars.

'I cannot lie. I was tempted, but also too scared to do it.'

Eventually it was agreed that Xie's money would be paid in four instalments. US$10,000 would be paid up front. Two payments of US$5,000 would be made when he reached Canada and America. If he could not agree to this, he would not go. Xie's uncle in America said he would cover the money in Canada and America up front. The last US$5,000 – to be paid within one year – would have to be earned by Xie, as would the US$10,000 – plus interest – that his uncle would expect back.

As his time to go drew nearer, Xie was apprehensive but also excited, as were his family. 'There were a few times I would have considered backing out, especially as I heard more and more about the accidents of boats sinking and so on, but people told me I would be fine – and besides I did not want to let my family down.'

As the day approached, he was told exactly what to take – and more importantly what not to. He was told to take the minimum of clothing, no more than one rucksack for everything. There would be food and water on the boat for him. If he wanted to take more food in his bag, that was up to him.

His worries had lessened when he learned that he would be travelling with two friends who were also opting to go by the same route.

When the day came, he remembers his father walking him out to the car that came to pick him up. His mother chose not to join them.

'My father told me that he was very proud of what I was doing and that he knew I would do well for myself. He gave me a slip of paper with a number for one of his brothers who had been in America for many years – the uncle who had said he would find me some employment and help look after me.'

The journey Xie and his friends took to the docks was uneventful. They were told that they would be put in a cargo container with 30 others, meaning 33 would be making the journey in the container. There would be a lot of other containers around them. They would be cocooned, but one side would face outwards and there would be some – not many – small holes for fresh air to come in.

Once a day, the container door would be opened briefly for some more air to get in and the toilets to be emptied. But the potentially new Americans had to stay quiet and not try to get out of the container because not everyone on the boat knew about the live cargo. Only a few knew, but they were never told if that included the captain.

It would take about 20 days to cross the Pacific and reach Canada, they were informed. From there they would be taken to America. As Xie's friends were going to New York – to the famed 'Golden Mountain' as New York's Chinatown is called – they would split up there, with Xie crossing by land to San Francisco while his friends used fake passports to fly to the USA.

In addition, they were instructed that, if they were caught, they had to claim they were fleeing for political purposes. And while the man behaved very matter-of-factly, that stopped as they neared the docks and were reminded who and what they were dealing with.

'He told us that if we had any plans about going our own way at any point,' Xie recalled, 'that he knew how to get in touch with our families here and abroad. He left us in no doubt that when he said "get in touch" he meant that they would be harmed if we did not pay back our loan at an acceptable rate, with money going to them monthly.'

They approached the large cargo boat at night and were quickly taken on board. Fear gripped Xie. 'I was suddenly terrified. Up until this point I had been caught up in what was happening but when I saw our container surrounded on the sides – and high above – by other containers, I started to get a feeling of claustrophobia, which was not helped when I looked into the container.

'It was dark with just a few lights on the sides. They seemed to be powered by a small generator, which also powered what looked to be a small heater. The only other things in the container – though to me it was little more than a box as it seemed so small – were mattresses and buckets and bags next to them. The buckets were meant to be our toilets. The bags contained bottles of water and some food. Definitely not enough to survive on for any longer than a week. Not even half a week.'

Xie and his friends were among the last to arrive and as such had the mattresses nearest the container door – but furthest away from the heaters. Their small bags next to the beds appeared to have been pilfered from, but they did not know if this had been done by the others or if the meagre supplies meant for the bags had just ran out before things could be put in their bags.

The two men who had led them onto the boat, who appeared to be members of the crew, said they would be nearby until the boat cast off. A few hours later, just before dawn, the two men returned and started to shut the container, saying they would be back in a day or so. They reminded the people inside to remain quiet because if they were discovered the consequences could be very bad.

Going by cargo boat is one of the more common ways of getting into America from China as it can be one of the cheapest. However, as with every method of smuggling, you get what you pay for. While what Xie was about to go through would be bad, it was better than some trips where people were put in a container days before the container was even placed on the ship and then left there until arrival in a new land.

But Xie was travelling in squalor by comparison to others. For example, a group of ten caught in 1999 entering Canada walked out of their container wearing new clothes and with mobile phones. They had paid a lot more than Xie to ensure they had the chance to walk about the boat once or twice and also to be fed more regularly. They had also paid for passports. But all the money they had did them little good, as they were caught within minutes of coming out of the container.

Cargo boat was one of the easiest ways to smuggle people until the grounding of the *Golden Venture* off New York City in 1993, which prompted immigration and customs teams to improve their efforts at finding immigrants smuggled this way. Twelve of the 277 passengers aboard the *Golden Venture* died trying to swim ashore and many others were held in immigration centres and jails until 1997. There have been other deaths, including three in a container not unlike the one Xie was travelling in, discovered at Seattle's port in January 2000.

But Xie was trying not to think about that. He never actually realised they were under way, as there was no frame of reference. All he had was a constant, dull light shining at him from 40 feet away. At first he had thought that people would turn the light off so they could all sleep but, as he learned over the first few days, some people wanted it on all the time – as if it reassured them – and very few wanted to socialise or chat, so Xie and his friends kept themselves to themselves. As no one spoke, the noise stayed down and again, on the first few days, the container door was opened for an hour every day, letting some fresh air in and the stale air out, but no one was able to get in or out. On what seemed like the tenth day, the two men returned and said that the weather was getting bad so they might not be round at this part of the ship for a few days. They threw in some food – which Xie and his friends managed to get a lot of as they were nearest – and then sealed the container up again without letting a lot of the stale air out.

But they didn't seal the container properly and, as the winds picked up, there was a slight clanging noise as metal hit metal. There were also other noises echoing through the container from things hitting the other containers, and the containers moving slightly.

'It was terrifying,' recalls Xie. 'I couldn't shake the feeling that we were going to slide overboard and be trapped in the container until we suffocated or drowned. Every noise seemed deafening and I know I wasn't the only one who was scared.'

To make matters worse, rain and seaspray started coming in from the airholes and the improperly locked door. While they were never in danger of being flooded out – they hoped – their mattresses were soaked at the bottom and some of their food was ruined.

As the weather got worse, the trip got a lot choppier too, causing people to be sick, but that wasn't just because of the sea. Some of the buckets were full and the motion spilled them over, again causing their contents to slop onto mattresses all over the container.

This was the worst part of the trip. People started fighting among themselves, and taking each other's mattresses. No one came near Xie and his friends. Everyone else seemed to be there by themselves. Xie had safety in numbers.

It took five days for the weather to improve and by then the container stank. The air was barely breathable and some people had taken to trying to drink the water being washed in by the rain and spray. Of course as some of this was mixed with what was on the container floor – as well as being seawater – this left them in a worse condition. Also during this time the small power generator gave out, plunging them into virtual darkness and cold.

'I have never seen a dead body but the smell in that container cannot have been any worse than death. If any elderly people had been with us they would have died. By the time the container was reopened we were almost delirious. The sunlight blinded us and the men seemed to be looking at us strangely. It was only later we would realise why.

'They told us that they had very little food or water that they could give us now, but that we were nearly there, with less than a week to go. But they did say we could come onto deck for a few moments. While that was happening, we saw them give about half of us – including me and my friends – some more food. Just a small amount to put in our pockets, but not everyone got some.'

While the rest of the trip was disgusting – 'the air reeked from the smells that were now embedded in the mattresses' –

it passed without any great event and on the last day the two men arrived and pointed out a number of people. All the ones they had given extra food to, to be exact. These were brought to the front of the group and told to go round to the front of the boat, to pick up some boxes and start unloading. If anyone quizzed them, they were told to act stupid and pretend they did not understand.

When Xie asked about the others, he was told that they would be left in the container and unloaded that way. What few had realised was that it was an unmarked container, and bribes had passed hands on land so that it would be placed with another ship's containers. That way if the less able were discovered, it would be another boat that was investigated. If they weren't discovered, they would be sneaked out at nightfall.

Xie and company were told that, once they had carried some boxes, they were to go with one of the two men, who would make it look as if they were going into the city. People were coming and going from the docks all the time, so no one would pay them any attention unless they acted suspiciously. The most important thing, they were told, was to act weary (something Xie didn't think would be too hard) and not look about them as if they were excited to be there.

'We were especially told not to look up as apparently only tourists do that', and that was what always tipped off the immigration people milling around the docks.

After they left the docks, they walked down a couple of streets into a bar that was teeming with Asians. The man behind the bar gave the boatman a nod and then led them all upstairs to a room.

Here, the boatman told them that they would have to stay over for a day or two, but some would leave sooner than others, all to go their separate ways. That night again, they slept on mattresses, but at least they were clean mattresses and everyone had the chance to shower and put on clean clothes that were provided for them. Phone calls were also made to ensure that money went to the snakeheads. Xie's uncle had transferred the money to Xie's parents days earlier so that went without a hitch.

The next morning Xie bade farewell to his friends as he was taken down to a car and driven to Windsor at the Niagara Falls. He was told that he would be put in the boot and they would have to time it so that they went when it was busy, as that was when you had least chance of being stopped.

In the boot, for the next two hours, Xie shivered in a nervous darkness, not knowing what was going on. At times the claustrophobia threatened to overwhelm him but he managed to control it. All he could feel was the stop-start of the car as it moved along.

Then there was a thump on top of the boot. Xie jumped with a start, banging his head on the underside of the boot. He knew then that he had given himself away and he sighed deeply as the boot was opened. To his pleasant surprise, it was the driver of the car standing over him, smiling. They had made it. Xie could now get in the front of the car and be driven to San Francisco.

The rest of the journey was completely uneventful. When they reached Chinatown, he was driven to another safehouse, from where his uncle was phoned and told to come get him once he had the money required. He turned up within a few hours.

As Xie left, he was reminded that he still had US$5,000 to pay and it would be collected from him monthly. There was no need for them to state what would happen if he didn't have the money.

His uncle was understanding about it. He told Xie that he could pay off the snakeheads before he worried about paying him back but, all in all, it looked as if Xie would be paying back about US$500 a month to people for around three or four years.

Xie paid off the snakeheads and is now working through his uncle's debt as well as sending money home. 'I am glad I came here. I am earning more money than I was back home. I am having to work long days – sometimes more than 20 hours – working for my uncle and others, but it is allowing me to have a lot of money for myself and my family, and I will build myself up. I know I will not be at the bottom of the ladder forever and I may be able to bring over either my family or perhaps a bride if I do not meet one here, but when you work so long it is hard to meet others.

'But I have no regrets about coming here. It was hard, yes, but I have made it.'

Xie's two friends who made the journey to New York were also successful in their border crossing, but some of their friends who opted to go to England a number of months later were not as fortunate and, if anything, their journey was even worse.

The journey from China to Britain, like the trip to America, varies in cost – starting at US$20,000 – depending on what you can afford and how quickly you want to be there. In one of the finest examples of cross-border cooperation seen, gangs from the Far East, mainland Europe and the UK all work together to try to ensure safe delivery of their cargo.

In Europe, the UK sees the largest amount of illegal immigrants from the Far East. Unofficial figures suggest that as many as the 1,500 of the 2,400 caught on a monthly basis hiding in freight lorries are Asian, again with the vast majority of them being from Fujian

Xie's friend Ying was one such person. Like Xie she opted for a cheap package, but she wanted to go to the UK. Some of her friends had gone there and she had more family there than she did in the USA, so she made the decision to leave in late 1999 and was all set to go in late May or early June the following year.

First of all, she travelled to Beijing before flying via Moscow to Belgrade in Yugoslavia with another group posing as tourists. Belgrade was chosen because the Chinese do not need a visa to reach there. No one gave them a second look. After all, more than 40,000 Chinese go there every year, using it as a staging post to elsewhere.

When they reached Belgrade, their Chinese passports were taken from them and replaced with fake Korean ones. Ying was also made to pose as a wife to one of the men seeking to flee to the UK.

The group then split up. Some made a journey that involved flying from Belgrade to Jordan and then going to Rome and Heathrow and getting off wherever they wanted to.

For others, including Ying, the journey was to prove a little more difficult. From the Balkans, the group of illegal immigrants was split and taken by sea – or overland – into Hungary, through Austria and into France, hidden in the backs of vans. Some of them left at France to be smuggled in that way and the rest boarded a train to get to the Netherlands, where they were handed over to the European side of the network, in Rotterdam. The complete journey took just under three weeks.

At Rotterdam, they were told that they would be put in a van, taken to Zeebrugge in Belgium, put on a ferry and then taken to Dover in England. Once they were past customs checkpoints, associates of the people in Rotterdam would then greet them.

The van was cramped, full of fruit crates on all sides – 'to help block any scanners', they were told – and they were warned that they had to be incredibly quiet.

They were not comfortable but they endured these conditions as they knew the marathon trip was nearly over. They had a rough idea of when they were moving and when they were not. When they heard the back doors being opened and crates being moved, they thought it was the end of their journey.

It wasn't. They had another long journey to face – back home. They had been caught. If they had left China at any other time, perhaps they would have made it, but the van had made the journey just over one week after Western Europe's biggest human-trafficking disaster, when 58 would-be migrants were found dead on a lorry at Dover.

It was the case that brought the problem of trafficking to the world's attention. Only two people – Su Di Ke, aged 20, and Ke Shi Guang, 22 – survived from the group of 56 men and four women who had set out to reach the UK for a better life. They had all paid £17,700 to reach the UK.

It transpired that they had died because of a closed air vent that resulted in heat exhaustion and no air entering the lorry. The two survivors were the last to have been loaded into the container and lay with their heads on the floor by the wooden partitions as the air ran out.

Police in Europe and the UK moved quickly to arrest the people involved and the subsequent trial gave an idea of the conditions the illegal immigrants had gone through. In Britain, the lorry driver Perry Wacker faced 58 charges of manslaughter as well as smuggling charges, all of which he

denied. And Chinese interpreter Ying Guo denied conspiracy to smuggle immigrants into Britain.

The court heard that Wacker drove the lorry to
Zeebrugge, leaving at 3 pm and arriving just after 6 pm.
After parking the lorry on the ferry Wacker went upstairs,
where he tucked into a meal and watched two films. The
immigrants were trapped inside the airtight container on
one of the hottest days of 2000 until the lorry was searched
at Dover at 11.43 pm.

Su Di Ke told the court that people noticed the lorry's air
vent was closed and started to get frightened halfway
through the six hours' crossing time of their ferry from
Zeebrugge. Sobbing in court, he said: 'They started pan-
icking after about two to three hours because the vent was
shut and there was no air. Some people removed tomatoes
and wanted to kick open the doors. There was also a lot of
shouting and screaming but nobody came to help and I fell
unconscious during all the panic.'

Ke Shi Guang had left China to practise his Catholic religion. He claimed that five or six hours into the journey
from Rotterdam to England he saw a man's hand closing
the air vent from outside. He also recalled: 'When we left
Rotterdam we were given four buckets of water to last the
journey but it was finished quickly. I did not have time to
get any.'

As the air ran out and the temperatures rose during the
crossing, the immigrants stripped to their underwear,
sucked the juice from the tomatoes and tried in vain to prise
open the air vent.

Fellow Chinese illegal immigrant Feng He told the jury
in the trial how he paid the equivalent of 24 years' salary to
be smuggled into Britain. He also added details about what
it took to get to the UK, describing a similar journey to that

of the doomed lorry. 'The lorry was very big. It was very dark and you could not see. It was lacking oxygen and I had difficulty breathing.'

Freight supervisor Barry Betts painted the most graphic picture of all. He said: 'When I got to the area, people were already unloading boxes. I could clearly see the body of a young Chinese man where the boxes had been, possibly a teenager. Myself and freight supervisor Darren Bailey got inside and I can remember it was very hot, when refrigerated containers carrying fruit are normally cold. We were clearing tomatoes from around this male's body and, as I shone my torch in and peered past the wooden structures holding up the boxes into the darkness, I was confronted by a sea of bodies, which all appeared to be motionless. I could see a young boy who was tapping the side of the container to try to attract our attention.

'I remember seeing another young man moving and he began climbing over other bodies to get to us. When he did we helped him out. It was clear there was no one else alive.'

The court also heard that Ying Guo destroyed her mobile phone after her number was found on some of the dead immigrants. It also turned out that Miss Guo had called case worker Chandika Walpita on the morning the asylum seekers were due to arrive at Dover, to ask if he could take on all 60 asylum claims. She later called him in a 'hysterical' state to say that her mobile phone number had been found on one of the bodies. Miss Guo's number was found on 27 of the bodies and on 16 items discarded in the back of the lorry.

Mr Walpita said, 'She told me that she had been instructed to ask about some Chinese asylum seekers who had arrived in the country. She said that there were 60 of them and asked whether I wanted to represent them. She had never said such numbers before. I said I wouldn't be able to take the whole lot but I said I might be able to take half.'

Miss Guo called him back 14 minutes later to say she was unsure what was happening with the immigrants. But Mr Walpita told the court he did not hear from her again until after midnight on 20 June.

'She said that they had found her mobile phone number on one of the persons who had been found dead in the container,' he said. 'She asked me what to do and I said I had no idea about criminal matters but that I could ask somebody who did. She said she had thrown her phone away, that she had destroyed it. She was a bit hysterical so I thought I wouldn't inquire any further as to why.'

Miss Guo called Mr Walpita once more in an anxious state, the court heard, to say she had been unable to contact the legal representative he had recommended. He said, 'She was anxious about something, worried.'

As well as throwing away her phone, it turned out that she had wiped records from her computer. The files included records of a Midland Bank account in Marble Arch, London.

Wacker was found guilty of 58 charges of manslaughter, as well as four counts of conspiracy to smuggle immigrants into the UK, and sentenced to 14 years in prison – eight years for conspiracy, and six years for manslaughter. Guo was jailed for six years for conspiring to smuggle illegal immigrants into Britain. And a Rotterdam court found seven others guilty of gross negligence over the deaths, but cleared them of manslaughter. Among nine defendants, two ringleaders – Gursel Ozcan and Haci Demir – were sentenced to nine years in jail. Five others received sentences of between 30 months and seven years, while two were acquitted. The judge said no punishment could make good the deaths of so many victims, and human trafficking led to the 'abuse of the desperate'.

Eight of the nine defendants belonged to a criminal organisation involved in illegal trafficking of immigrants and forgery. One of the eight was acquitted of all charges, along with a ninth person who had been accused only of forgery. The prosecution at the Rotterdam court had requested prison sentences ranging from six months to 20 years but these were scaled back when it was learned that the European mainland authorities could possibly have prevented the deaths by intervening earlier, when they first learned of the cargo.

However, none of the sentences could bring back the dead – or help the illegal immigrants who had been captured after the case, including Ying. Ying was sent back home where, according to Xie, she is paying back what she still owes from that failed attempt before she saves up to start a fresh effort to begin a new life.

Xie just hopes that new life isn't in the afterlife.

2

COMING TO AMERICA

America, land of the free – for some anyway. Many others want it to be the land of their freedom. It is not just the Chinese who are fascinated with North America. People from practically every other nation want to try to get into the USA. Post-11 September 2001 worries about it being a target again have not deterred those who want the dream of the dollar and Mom's American pie, believing the inscription upon New York's Statue of Liberty as written by Victorian Emma Lazarus:

> Give me your tired, your poor,
> Your huddled masses yearning to breathe free,
> The wretched refuse of your teeming shore,
> Send these, the homeless, tempest-tossed to me:
> I lift my lamp beside the golden door.

And it's not just one or two people trying to get in the golden door, either. It is believed that more than 10,000 people try to get into America by land or sea on a nightly basis. The odds are in their favour because the US Border Patrol cannot be everywhere, having to cover the 6,000 miles of Mexican and Canadian international land borders and 2,000 miles of coastal waters – including the Florida peninsula and the island of Puerto Rico – with only 125 aircraft and 88 sea vessels.

The agents are still relatively successful in their work, though. For example in 2001, border patrol agents apprehended just under 1.2 million people for illegally entering the country.

But many more still get in. A survey in 2002, carried out by the Washington, DC-based Center for Immigration Studies, suggested that there were perhaps as many as 8.7 million illegal aliens in the country. This did not include the 2.7 million who were given amnesty and legal permanent residence in 1986 in an effort to combat the problem.

However, scholars at Boston's North-Eastern University have suggested that the actual number might be as high as 13 million when the fact that polls and census results rarely manage to include everybody is taken into account, while Harvard Professor George Borjas claims some economists put the net cost of immigration at US$70 billion a year.

Canada is the more popular choice for those coming from abroad but Mexico's border with America sees nightly tides of Mexicans trying to get over. There are a suspected 4.5 million Mexican immigrants in the USA, and many more want to be there. While most Mexicans cross over for the money – more than US$1 billion is believed to be sent back to Mexico every year from Mexicans working in the USA – it has now reached the stage where many attempt to go over because all their friends have tried it. In other parts of the world, immigration can be seen as a problem; in Mexico it is pandemic.

The biggest problem – for the Americans – is the size of the border. Despite modern technology and manpower they cannot stop every vehicle or be at every spot along its 2,100-mile length. Vehicles alone are a big problem. More than 45,000 vehicles per week cross the border, half of them at just one spot – the San Ysidro border crossing in San Diego.

People trying to get into North America have three options – they can bluff it out in a car, they can hide in a vehicle or they can walk through mountains and on to freedom. All are popular choices.

By far the easiest is the old-fashioned bluff of just going through and hoping not to be stopped. The next step up is to show a card known as a *matriculas*, which has a person's details, including name and address. These cards allow for crossing the border and as such are highly desirable for people to get their hands on. To get one, Mexican nationals must show a certified copy of their birth certificate and an official photo ID, such as a Mexican driver's licence, voter registration card or a school ID. They also must show proof of an address in the United States, such as a lease or utility bill.

These cards may only cost US$29 legally, but to get one that leaves no traces can cost upwards of US$100 as they can be quite tricky to forge – not that that stops there being a flood of poor fakes.

'I've seen everything from poor photocopies to quite expensive-looking copies. It's the crap ones that get your attention, though, as they stick out so obviously and you almost feel insulted as if "You thought I would fall for this?"' said retired border guard Hank Mitchell. 'And to be fair,' he added, 'some of them might have got through. With the volume of traffic you're dealing with, you don't always have the luxury of time.'

The time problem is what also makes the next option so appealing – that of hiding in the vehicle. While powerful X-ray machines help by revealing details of what is in a vehicle, not every vehicle can be X-rayed or even manually searched. But sometimes people being smuggled in give themselves away – as did Enrique Aguilar Canchola. He was sewn into an empty car seat, only to be found because the US customs inspector noticed two legs sticking out of the unoccupied seat. While it affords amusing mental images, this is one of the more dangerous ways of sneaking into the USA.

Migrants try to gain entry to the United States by hiding in hollowed-out gasoline tanks, by strapping themselves to undercarriages and by cramming themselves into a small space that smugglers have made in an engine or behind a dashboard.

Hank Mitchell remembers one of the first times he saw one: 'I was searching this car and it seemed fine, until I opened the glove compartment and there was a face staring back at me. At first I thought it was just a head until it started speaking to me. I can't tell you what was going through my head. It totally shook me up – you do not expect to see a talking head in a glove compartment!'

As with all things involving smuggling, the smugglers' techniques are becoming more and more complicated. False walls and so on are almost passé in the business. One said, 'I found immigrants in the twin, hollowed-out gasoline tanks of a pick-up truck, breathing through regulators connected to oxygen bottles next to the driver. Some of the things they come up with are ingenious.'

And the ingenious schemes – some of which would not be out of place in a James Bond film – are on the rise. In the first five months of 2001, inspectors at San Ysidro recorded 1,236 cases involving migrants hidden in vehicle boots or hidden compartments, up 43 per cent from 862 cases in the same time period in 2000, according to the Immigration and Naturalisation Service (INS).

When he was captured, Enrique was quite calm about who was to blame for it all. 'If they hadn't doubled the number of border patrol agents and put in more fences, lights and sensors along the border we wouldn't have to try these things.'

And while Enrique – who, according to Hank, is captured roughly once a week – cannot legally return for five years, Hank is in no doubt that border guards will be seeing him before then.

'You have to remember that these people do not set out to get caught. Also, people like Enrique, who have been caught often, think that this is the time they will get through. The funny thing is that for every long-timer like Enrique, there are people who get through on their first attempt.'

Border patrol agents are finding an increasing number of illegal aliens loaded onto flatbeds (a truck where the trailer is part of the vehicle). In South Texas alone, agents found 711 illegal immigrants in 36 flatbeds during 2001, but 799 had been found in 56 flatbeds by August 2002.

There have been no deaths in Texas but immigrants elsewhere along the border were not so lucky. In Dallas on 27 July 2002, two immigrants died after being locked in a flatbed for 12 hours with no water or ventilation.

But it's not just flatbeds that are used. On 31 July 2002 about 32 illegal aliens were found in a trailer at San Antonio, and in early August 2002, 73 illegal aliens were found hidden in a trailer that was stopped at the Sarita checkpoint about 60 miles north of Brownsville.

According to a spokesman for the border patrol, people are coming across in larger and larger groups. This is not because they all know each other, but because this is the way that immigrants are being forced to do it by the people masterminding the smuggling.

Increased security along the border not only boosted the number of people being smuggled in through vehicles, but it also forced others to make the treacherous trip through the mountains and deserts, which are more remote and harder to be tracked through. The results have been fatal, as the death toll of immigrants is reaching record rates in the most remote and dangerous outposts.

August 2002 was the deadliest month to date for the south-west border, with 100 migrants known to have died in one sector alone, and more than 2,000 dead since 1994. The Mexican Government believes that at least two people a day die and are buried in America while trying to cross the border.

While many people have suffocated in airless trucks, died in vehicle crashes, been struck by lightning or drowned, the most common causes of death are heatstroke or dehydration – especially in the mountains or desert.

'A single human being couldn't carry the water needed to survive in this desert,' said one border patrol agent, pointing out that as well as distance and rough terrain, there is heat – up to 129 degrees Celsius – blistering winds, poisonous snakes, and mountains.

Migrant organisations blame the border patrol for the mounting deaths, saying that its decision to focus its policing on border cities has driven migrant traffic to the most severe terrain, something that the patrol denies. But at the same time a spokesman for the patrol has pointed out that welfare of illegal immigrants is not their main job.

'Our primary mission is to protect our nation's borders,' said Mario Villarreal, a spokesman for the border patrol in Washington, DC, in June 2002. To try to stop people from dying from dehydration, the Mexican social security administration now hands out a survival kit for immigrants, including antidotes for snake bites, rehydration tablets, first-aid materials and dried foods to use on protracted crossings.

The USA was not happy about this, claiming it looked as though the Mexican Government was helping people to cross the border, but Mexican officials said that was not the case and it was just trying to keep the fatalities down.

Fire is also another problem. Immigrants being forced to try new routes increases the risk of wildfires breaking out. In 2002 more than 300 fires ravaged the area along the USA–Mexico border, and fire officials in Southern California put the blame squarely on illegal immigrants from nearby Mexico. They expect many more in the years to come.

But the risks do not deter everyone. Twenty-one-year-old Eugenio was one such person. The dark-skinned, athletic young man did not want to move to America from Guatemala City forever, only for some months each year. Life had been hard for his family – including his mother and three sisters – since their father had died, ironically because of border crossing.

'My dad had moved from Guatemala City and worked as a "coyote" – one of the people who help get people across the border – but one night he was shot by a group patrolling the border. The people with him told us that it wasn't the guards but one of the vigilante groups that go about. The rest of them were captured by border guards as they tried to escape the shooters. They were brought back here and told us what had happened, but I don't know if the Americans did anything with the group.'

Eugenio had one advantage over many people – his dad's knowledge. 'He had taught me a lot, including not to give in if I'm caught the first time. I just wanted to work here about eight months and then take the money home to my family, and then do that every year, working more if it was needed. I was quite content where I was in Guatemala City but someone had to provide for my family.'

Eugenio's family would be allowed to continue a decent life if he could get to the USA and earn US$200 per week – not a fortune but far more than the US$30 per week he made at home. Eugenio's plan was that from Guatemala City he would transfer to a bus headed for the Mexican border, which is not the usual route people take, but Eugenio knew that the higher expense of this route could prove cheaper in the long run:

'People usually cross at Tecún Umán, or Talismán, but a lot of people are robbed and assaulted there. You also have to know who to trust. It's not uncommon for some coyotes to sell their people at the border or take people into the countryside where they take whatever they have and abandon them. Many guides turn out to be *bajadores* or bandits and they rob you. And if you have nothing to rob, then they beat you up out of anger.'

However, a major problem occurred when the bus driver died the day before the journey was due to take place. This forced Eugenio to cross at Tecún Umán. He paid a *valsero* (ferryman) two pesos to cross the Suchiate River on an inner-tube raft. From there, he went on, to one of the most dangerous parts of the journey – more dangerous than the actual crossing into the USA – at Tapachula, Mexico. This is where many migrants are caught by the Mexican *migra* (immigration agents/border patrol). Illegals are not just put on a bus and sent back to Guatemala, they are also robbed of all their possessions – and sometimes their nicer clothes – before being sent back.

Using information from both his dad and his dad's contacts, Eugenio made it past Tapachula and into Veracruz, zigzagging east before straightening his course towards Mexico City. There he gambled in shady bars and back-streets until he was able to 'persuade' someone to pass on a copy of their Mexican birth certificate, which could prove handy if he was stopped by Mexican authorities. Eugenio spent some time in Mexico City, befriending others who were planning the leap across to North America. This, he openly admits, was not out of concern for them, but rather pragmatism on his part.

'If three or four people try and cross the border and the guards catch three of the four, they will be pleased with that haul. I was working on that basis. It was not nice, but I was not doing this out of kindness for anyone else. I was doing this for my family.'

As they approached the border, Eugenio discovered the worst thing possible. The information on the map he had was out of date. Where there should have been nothing more than a fence, there was a brick concrete wall.

'I hadn't thought that there was a reason the maps we had at home were not with my father. Of course I realised it there and then – it was because they were old maps. All his useful maps had been on his body when he died and, like his body, they were never returned to us.'

It was too late to turn around. The group of four decided to go for it. They helped each other up and over the wall and dropped to the other side. And were caught.

'All I remember from that,' says Eugenio, 'is the bright searchlights dazzling us. It was incredible. Two of us tried to run but we couldn't see and ran straight into border patrol guards. We were all handcuffed, put on a bus and taken to Agua Prieta back in Mexico after they had checked us out.

'One of the men with me said I was pretty stupid to have my Mexican birth certificate with me, but what that meant was that I would be dropped off in Mexico and they wouldn't try to send me directly back home. I knew I did not sound very Mexican in the way I spoke, so I needed the certificate.

'We were warned never to try this again and told we were getting off lightly. The others looked as if they had heard this all before and just an hour after we were off the bus, we were already considering starting off again.'

This time, Eugenio fell in with some people who were being packed onto pick-up trucks with cattle cages on the back. They were leaving the next night. He was told he would be travelling *encebollados* – onion style – where you are laid down side by side, with one person's head going one way and the next person's head going the other way. A second layer of people lay across the others in the same way. Then the smugglers bolted a sheet of plywood on top of the truck bed. It is not a pleasant way to be smuggled over but it can be cheap. However, it is dangerous and, as they approached the border, the trip became too much for one woman.

'One of the women began to cry. She was told by one of the others that if she made any sound along the way she would be taken out and killed, which only made her more hysterical, and we were caught.

'Again, we were all taken back to Agua Prieta and dumped there. I spent a few days there, raising some more money in gambling – mostly taking it from other people trying to cross the border – until I had enough to make one more attempt at crossing.'

One week after his previous attempt, Eugenio went into a van with 20 others and was driven west on Highway 2 towards Naco. This was the most dangerous route he had tried to date as it would involve crossing desert and mountains known as Las Antenas where many others had died, normally from heatstroke or dehydration. Eugenio recalls that, at the last moment, people changed their mind.

'They took us into the mountains and dropped us off at the end of this road and told us to start walking. Two people begged to be taken back – afraid they could not do it – and they were taken back, though no money was returned to them. The rest of us set off. It was a hard walk, and within only a few hours many people had used all of the one gallon of water they had been given.

'We joined up with another group who were on the second day of their walk, and we all refilled our water containers from a cache of bottles the smugglers had planted along the route. I had heard good things about the people who had arranged this trip and I was pleased that it was going well with water because that is the biggest problem. You cannot carry all your water on a trip this long and need to resupply at points.'

By the third night of walking, the illegal entrants and their guides had covered more than 15 miles, over mountain ranges in Mexico to the southern edge of the Mule Mountains in Arizona. The weather had started to turn for the worse, so they decided to rest in the brush, a quarter-mile south of the highway to Bisbee.

And then they were caught. Again.

However, the border patrol guard couldn't fit all of the people into the van in one go. Nor could he get any back-up, so he took some and told the rest to stay, assuming the bad weather would force them to stay there. He was wrong.

Eugenio and two others took their chance, running to where they hoped the highway was. Eugenio was in luck because the two people he had run with were two of the guides. Not only did they know the way, but they also knew how to get away. They used a phone they had with them to ask a contact from Bisbee to come to collect them, which he did, hiding them in the boot of his vehicle until he got them to the garage of a safe house.

Bisbee is not the safest place to be in because there are still immigration checkpoints but Eugenio managed to convince the men to try to get him on a flight to Phoenix.

'It got to the stage where I had convinced them that, as I was the only one who had made it from the group, they were still getting value for money. I also pointed out to them that as I was not going into my father's trade then that was less competition for them. In the end I think they helped me just to be rid of me and because it was less hassle than taking me back.'

Eugenio had to go through a slight makeover to make the final stage of the journey; dressing to try to look more American. He was driven along Highway 80 to Sky Harbour. After that, it was a case of getting to San Francisco, which he eventually managed. Within days he had succeeded in getting a factory job, where he met some fellow countrymen. They took him under their wing, telling him to learn English quickly so that he could earn more money. He found this a problem, 'because everyone speaks Spanish in the groups I was in and not English as I expected.'

He now lives with ten other people, which helps keep his living costs down. He works six days a week, earning US$350, most of which is sent back home in one of few non-working rituals Eugenio has in his new land.

After being paid for his work every Saturday, Eugenio stops at the travel agency he uses to wire money to his family. It's a small shop, with signs in its windows advertising airfares to places in South American countries. He counts out US$180 and passes the bills across the counter to an employee. He pays the woman a fee of US$9.20.

The next day, back in Guatemala City, Eugenio's family take a bus to an office where they are given the money sent every week. It is quickly divided up into what it is to be used for, and his mother smiles and thanks God for her son being so loyal and dedicated that he is working away to help provide for them. She also looks forward to the day her son will come back, when she can thank him in person.

And that is the only sad note in the tale. For while the mother is happy and the son is delighted to be able to provide, there is no certainty Eugenio can return.

'I would have to smuggle myself out of America and back in, which could prove dangerous as well as expensive. It may work out better for now to just keep working and hope that something can be worked out in the future. For now I am happy to make sure that my family have a good life. They deserve it.'

But, as pointed out earlier, not everyone finds it so difficult to get into the country, especially if they can afford a plane flight and a visa. Kaitlyn Andrews was 28 when she decided to go over to America for a holiday to help get over her break-up with her fiancé. She planned to stay for a month or so before heading back home to Dublin, but she started to feel herself being seduced by the American dream and life in the States.

'After six weeks were up I'd grown to love the lifestyle and didn't want to go home. I knew I'd become an illegal immigrant but I pushed that to the back of my mind. I was hoping that if I didn't think about it, it wouldn't exist.'

While many people may find that hard to believe, the fact that Kaitlyn saw many other illegal immigrants made it a lot easier.

'Besides, Americans don't seem to have as much of a problem with white-looking people as they do with non-white people trying to get into America. I knew lots of people in the same boat as me and none of them had been caught. It was easy not to think about it and there was so much fun to be had. Also, no one thinks of themselves as a criminal. I know I didn't.

'One of the things I had to do, though, was find work. The first job I got was as a roller-skating waitress in a theme bar called Hooters. I did that for two years. Then I became a sales consultant for a very funky clothes designer, travelling back and forth from coast to coast all over America.

'As my wages had to be paid straight into a bank account, I persuaded a friend to get me a fake social security number, which was fairly easy to come by. Again, a lot of people don't see that as breaking the law because so many people do it. And the companies hiring you just assume you have a Green Card because you've been in the States for so long and you have come from previous jobs.

'At one time someone did try to help me get a work permit but it was such a long-winded procedure that I stupidly gave up on it, thinking that I wouldn't be bothered by things or caught. I had no intention of leaving the country, so how were immigration officers going to find me?

'Also, you tell yourself that you're going to get round to doing it one day, but other things keep getting in the road.'

The main thing that kept getting in the road for Kaitlyn was fun.

'I really was living the dream. I earned good money and had a fantastic lifestyle. I moved into a beautiful apartment in Beverly Hills. I had nine great girlfriends, ten pairs of Gucci shoes and a wardrobe full of designer clothes. Every Friday the ten of us girls would hire a limo and hit LA hotspots where we would see stars like Matt Damon, Ben Affleck and George Clooney. That happened so often that we'd take no notice of them. It was an incredible life, far removed from the one I had in Dublin. I had never thought that life could be so much fun and so full of variety.

'But there was the one downside – I couldn't return to Ireland because I wouldn't have been allowed back into the USA again. The way round that, of course, was that my friends and family came over here. Some of them knew the truth but the rest of them just thought that I had been going through the process of getting work permits and so on.

'My mum and dad had been really worried for me but when they came over and saw how I was living and what my friends were like, they were reassured. I come from a big family so every couple of months someone else was over seeing me and I'm sure my parents were getting complete reports on everything. I wrote, emailed and called home a lot, so that helped.

'I spent two years just having a great time. I was seriously considering just staying here the rest of my life. That decision had been made earlier, when I had met Josh, but after a year he told me that he wanted to take things slower than they had been going – I think he had been afraid that I would want to get married. That really hurt me, but after a few months we drifted back together and life seemed to be going well.'

But, as so often happens, it's when life seems at its happiest that something comes along to ruin it.

'I had five major clients in San Diego who I'd visit on a fortnightly basis with new clothes, as I was working as a clothes advisor to some shop owners. I'd take a selection of garments and they'd always snap them up. Usually I shared the journey with another girlfriend who sold a different line of merchandise, but she'd dropped out of this trip because she had the flu. I'd just finished visiting the last store and was anxious to get back to LA as Josh and I had planned a romantic weekend.

'Fifteen minutes out of town on Freeway 5 I was approaching what's known as the San Diego Checkpoint. It was set up to prevent illegal produce being smuggled in from Mexico but it's also used for sifting out illegal aliens attempting to cross the border.

'I learned later that on this particular day the authorities were on the lookout for single girls who were being used to traffic marijuana across the border. Of course, I had no contraband on me at all, only a line of designer clothes. But it was my bad luck that I was travelling alone on that occasion – it made me of more-than-usual interest to the customs officials.

'As our cars were edging towards the checkpoint, I began to feel nervous. I got a sense of foreboding, which had never happened before. I must have had "guilty" written all over my face. Suddenly there was a tap on the window. I started shaking – not the right thing to do with a US immigrations officer breathing down your neck.

'He asked me if I was an American citizen and I replied that I was. I've no idea what possessed me to say that. I don't know if I was thinking that he would let me go if I said "Yes" or if I actually half-thought I was because I had been there so long.

'He then asked if I had any papers or ID. I said, "No". They then started to search the car and found my passport in the glove compartment. The officer checked the name and number on his radio and found out that I had entered the country in 1998 and hadn't officially exited.

'They hadn't found a drug trafficker but they'd nabbed an illegal alien. A woman officer grabbed my arm and handcuffed me. I was taken away to be fingerprinted, and then I was led to a cold, concrete-floored room with a filthy loo in the corner and a narrow bench with a dirty blanket. By turns the officers were either nice or nasty. I was so alone and very scared.

'After an hour, I was allowed to make phone calls. I tried three friends but none of them were in. It felt like my whole world had collapsed. I was freezing as I was still in the skimpy top and flip-flops I'd been arrested in. I was told that I'd probably get bail in the morning and, feeling slightly better but totally exhausted, I lay down on the hard bench and tried to get some sleep. I'd just managed to doze off when at about 3 am I was woken up and handcuffed again to be escorted to another holding area.

'On this trip I was in the middle of five male prisoners. While I was in the van I noticed that the prisoner sitting behind me was unshackled. He started reaching his arm round to maul me. Then to my horror he moved forward, squeezed into the seat next to me and started stroking my arm. He was feigning concern but I was terrified he was going to rape me while the officers in the front turned a blind eye. I called out to them but they either couldn't hear my cries for help or callously chose to ignore them. It was a horrendous ordeal. Thank God the journey to the next holding cell was just half an hour.

'Over the next few days I was led from one filthy detention centre to another, always without notice – just handcuffed and removed. On the third day, with no information coming through despite a visit from an attorney, I was manacled again and taken to a mixed prison, with horrors of clanging gates and people wailing and shouting obscenities. There were men in one wing and women in another.

'If I'd felt low up until then, now I was desolate. I had no idea when I'd be leaving or where I was going to go when I did. Now I know that my parents back home in England [her parents had moved there from Ireland] were having a dreadful time, unable to get any information about me and hearing stories third- and fourth-hand that left them in despair. They were desperately trying to get a copy of my birth certificate and a recent photo sent to the States to prove I actually was the person I was purporting to be.

'Upon arrival at the penitentiary I was stripped, searched and put into prison clothes. It was terrifying. Nothing prepares you for the reality of prison in a foreign country. When I thought of the cushioned life I'd led, I wondered if I'd ever get back to normality again.

'The very worst thing of all was the sanitation. In the prison there was only one loo in the middle of the room with no privacy at all. It was disgusting. There was no loo roll and it didn't flush properly. I just couldn't bring myself to use it and was constipated for a whole week.

'I did get access to the phone and everybody outside was incredibly supportive. I could tell they were desperately trying to get me out. A couple of times I was told I was getting bail. I'd prepare myself and feel a bit optimistic, but then it would be rescinded and I'd be back to square one.

'The frustration was unbearable. I wasn't allowed to make trans-Atlantic calls so I couldn't even speak to my mum. All I wanted was the comfort of my parents back home in England. Because of the British support for America's war on terror following September 11th, some of the wardens were very nice to me. But some said I'd be there for months.

'On the seventh day of my time I was taken from my cell, given my street clothes and handcuffed yet again. I thought

I was getting bail because it had been promised to me on and off for the previous 24 hours. But instead I was given my deportation papers and taken directly to San Diego airport to be put on a plane to London.'

Kaitlyn was told that she would not be allowed to go back to her apartment in Los Angeles to collect any personal belongings or say goodbye to her friends. She was also banned from returning to the USA until 2012. Despite all she has gone through, she has no hesitation when you ask her if she would return to the USA.

'In a moment,' she says. 'I don't think I would chance sneaking in – though I have been tempted – but I hope that I can get back. Josh and I have kept in touch and he says that he might come over here. Perhaps if we got married and stayed here until 2012 then the US authorities would see that we were a genuine couple and would allow me back in and, this time, I would stay legally.'

However, no one ever said leaving home and moving away was easy, under any circumstances. It can be a terribly distressing time, with the thought of a new life abroad seeming outweighed by the familiar life at home. Nevertheless, many still choose to go legally to America. There are a number of ways to do this. Many people apply for their paperwork before they get to the USA. Others try to organise it when they arrive, or upgrade their immigrant status once in the USA.

Just over 1 million people became legal immigrants to the USA in 2001, of who 411,059 received visas from US consuls overseas, while 653,259 collected their Green Cards in the US via Adjustment of Status. From that million, 179,195 came for jobs, while over 675,000 were relatives in one form or another of someone resident in the USA. Asylum seekers were the second lowest group arriving, with

108,506 refugees being allowed in. The last 42,015 were allowed in by America's visa lottery scheme.

Where do all these people go? More than half end up in one of the following states – California (282,957 people), New York (114,116), Florida (104,715), Texas (86,315), New Jersey (59,920) and Illinois (48,296).

And where are they all coming from? Five countries make up the largest figures – Mexico (206,426), India (70,290), China (56,426), the Philippines (53,154) and Vietnam (35,531). In comparison, Britons going to the US make up a tiny 18,000 – sixteenth in the list of nations, behind the likes of Cuba, Canada and Russia but in front of Columbia and Pakistan.

Joanne Murphy was a Briton who decided to go to the USA in the late 1990s after falling for her New York husband Kevin Brown, who she had met while on holiday. Having already had one bad marriage, Joanne decided that she wanted to start a new life in the USA.

The wedding was lovely, and Joanne was allowed to live in America while her Green Card application (citing family-based immigration, namely her husband) was considered. She hoped it would not take too long.

'I had originally been in the United States on a B2 visitor's visa, which lasted six months and had been quite easy to get. I was hopeful that getting into America for good would be as easy, but people said it would be anything but,' she remembers, laughing at her own innocence.

American immigration is a nightmare of form-filling, bureaucracy and red tape, but millions still put themselves through it. Joanne was able to come to America and work while waiting for the application to be processed after filing forms known as I–130 and having a non-immigrant K–3 Visa gained through a Form I–129F. Fortunately there were no children involved at that point or there would have been even more paperwork to fill out.

One of the reasons for this is that in the early 1980s, the INS found that half the petitions based on marriage were fraudulent, as the marriages were entered into solely for the purpose of obtaining Green Cards. Since then – with the backing of new laws – it has been heavily clamping down, adhering strictly to the letter of the law in an effort to make sure only true couples come to America. The authorities take the situation seriously, having made the matter a federal crime, which means that those found guilty can be imprisoned for up to five years or fined up to US$250,000, or both.

Joanne had to prove that she wanted to stay in the USA. One of the most important parts of this was the interview where she and her husband would be quizzed on a number of things. Before that, however, they had to fill out another myriad set of forms. A lot of documentation was required, including: birth certificates; health details, with physical reports; and identification documents such as driver's licence, employment ID, credit cards, current passport and Form I–94, Arrival Record, Social Security cards, leases on all apartments they had lived in (regardless of country) with rent receipts, hospital cards, union books, insurance policies, bank accounts, telephone, gas and electric bills or charge cards containing their details.

In addition, they also had to provide letters from employers; federal, state and city income tax returns, signed, dated and authenticated by the Internal Revenue Service; wedding pictures and anything else that would help show they were a loving couple. They were told that not all of these were essential, but that the more they had, the better.

Fortunately Joanne knew all of this before she left for America and was able to bring a lot of the necessary documents with her. However, she was mistaken in thinking that with those papers, the furniture she was having shipped over and her credit cards, she would be fine. It took a few months before she could really begin to settle down.

'America lives on credit ratings and histories. I thought I would be fine as I have VISA and Mastercard credit cards, which work worldwide. Nope. Not a chance.

'Technically, I was told, I was worse than bad credit because someone with bad credit can work it off and improve it – I had no credit whatsoever.

'Getting a bank account was slightly tricky too. Unlike the UK, US banks didn't seem to do credit checks but they did need a social security number – which I didn't have. That took a few trips – and more form-filling – to the nearest Social Security Administration office, who sent me out a number four weeks later.

'Bizarrely enough, even though I couldn't get a new credit card, I could still use my old credit cards. But I still had to deal with numbers and banks in the UK to pay them off, which was frustrating and expensive. What I later learned was that the best way to do it would have been to get either an American Express or a Diners card set up in England before I had left. For some reason these two companies can do transfers to an American address quite easily, but the others do not.

'Even though I was obviously living with Kevin, I wanted my own car and a telephone line for work for two reasons. First, I am a fairly independent woman and didn't see the point in him paying for me. Second, I wanted to build up my credit history.

'Another way of getting things going was to pay a card up in advance, like making a deposit, and then only being allowed to spend what I had – almost like using a Switch card. Many banks in America don't do overdrafts as easily as they do in the UK, but that wasn't a problem.

'What was a problem was equipment. After paying a fortune to get a lot of my stuff over, we discovered that it was all practically junk as America runs on a different electricity supply. I had thought all we would have to do would be to change plugs but it turns out that the UK voltage is almost twice that of America. Some computers can apparently make the switch, but my Macintosh couldn't, I was told. It was the same for the television (our signal is called PAL but theirs is NTSC), video and kitchen equipment. In fact the only thing I think that I kept was my discman!

'One thing I did while I wasn't working was to take and pass my driving test, as that at least gave me a form of identification, which was more than useful and at times made me feel like a legitimate person.'

The process was slow and months would go by without Joanne hearing anything.

'We had to get certain parts notarised. We had to make eight or nine copies of everything, paying for a lot of things. It was incredible! At times you just want to chuck it all in, especially when you hear about the illegal immigrants getting away with it.

'And I was convinced the reason I was being failed was because I had declared that once in the past I had a minor drugs offence when I was a teenager, and the silence was them watching me to see if I would offend again. I know it sounds very paranoid, but you hear of the people who get rejected and how strict the system is and you do get really really scared. Kevin and I got to the point that we wouldn't talk about it because we really didn't know what we would do if we were forced to split up.'

The long-awaited interview came one year after they had arrived in America to start their new life. While the receptionist before the meeting told them not to worry, Joanne couldn't help it.

'It only lasted about half an hour. The man asked us questions about what the other person liked and disliked, and our dates of births. He wanted to see pictures of us, and to know what I thought of America and so on.

'The one question that surprised us was when he asked if we argued and we replied differently. I said that we did and Kevin said we didn't. I thought that was us. Kevin then said that "Yes we did, but not a lot" and he didn't want to make us look like a divorce case. I also added in that "Yes, we had the odd row", but that I was the one who stewed on them, while Kevin – who sometimes didn't even realise we were arguing – never gave it a second thought.

'The man just laughed. He said that it was one of the questions that threw everyone, but that couples who looked suspicious always both said they never argued, as they always try to look too perfect. He always asks it now just to see the response. He then added that as long as we didn't keep arguing too much and stayed together, he didn't see a problem with me staying in the United States.

'It was an incredible feeling, one of total relief. At that moment I thought the USA was the greatest place on the planet.'

Joanne was told that she would be a permanent resident, but not a permanent, permanent resident! In America, there are two kinds of permanent resident – ones who are, well, permanent and ones who are called 'conditional permanent residents'.

Everyone is conditional for their first two years of getting their Green Card. Before the end of the two years they have to apply to the US Government for a change in status to permanent permanent. Failure to do so carries a hefty penalty – the authorities cancel immigration status (and that of any unmarried children the applicant may have had with their partner) and throw them out of the country.

This is because they assume that the reason for not reapplying to get the 'conditional' removed is that the marriage was entered fraudulently to obtain the Green Card. There are believed to be tens of thousands of people in America who are technically illegal immigrants because of the time slip.

However, Joanne's thought that America was the greatest country in the world did not last long. A few months later, she learned that her father had fallen ill back in the UK. She went back to spend time with and look after him in his last months. The illness dragged on, but he eventually passed away. Kevin came over to comfort her and they then tried to return to America. They did not get very far.

At immigration she was told that her residence had expired and she was sent back to the UK immediately. 'I was in tears, I had just lost my dad and now this. It was incredible.'

Kevin stayed in the USA, getting a lawyer who advised that Joanne would be able to return as a tourist while they fought what had happened. To their dismay they were told to begin the process again, though Joanne could stay temporarily as long as the matter was being sorted out.

Two years later Joanne heard that her mother was ill and, again, she left the USA for her mother's final days, this time leaving Kevin with Aaron and Emily, their children. On her return to the USA she was told that, because of her drug conviction and her breaking of the first residency conditions, she would not be allowed to stay. Her lawyer again fought this and she was granted another temporary residency permit. The authorities then began to try to remove her, a battle that had not been decided by May 2003. She has been warned that she may face a wait of another 12 months at least to get it sorted out. For Joanne, the American dream is tarnished.

'I can't believe how it ended up and how callous parts of the system seem to be. We have provided them with medical statements on a number of things – including the facts that my parents had terminal illnesses – but it doesn't seem to have done much good. As much as anything now, I'm worried for the children. This is the only home they have and I don't want to move them from it. Our lawyer is hopeful that we may either get lost in the system – which I doubt – or that compassion may be shown to us on humanitarian grounds. In the meantime, all we can do is hope and be a family for as long as we can.'

3

CAMPED OUT IN AUSTRALIA:
GOING NATIVE IN A LAND OF IMMIGRANTS

Australia, like America, is a land made strong in modern times by immigrants – and perhaps the butchery of its ethnic races. The romantic myths tell of people, mostly prisoners, coming to Australia and converting it from a barren land to a nation that most of the world envies for lifestyle, architecture, weather and perceived laid-back, non-aggressive attitudes to everything.

Of course, anything that attractive is going to attract a lot of people, some of whom will do anything to get into the country.

Since colonisation, immigration has continued to play an important part in Australia's history. Before World War 2, Britain was traditionally its main source of immigrants. After the war, the country wanted up to 100,000 immigrants per year and hunted all over Europe for them, with the emphasis on people with white skin and blue eyes. This was known as the 'White Australia' policy, which ended in 1975. Coincidentally this was the year the Vietnam War ended, and many Vietnamese refugees fled to the country.

In the 1980s emigration to Australia saw more Chinese than ever before join the country, as business emigrants were targeted, with the largest number coming from China, Malaysia and Indonesia. Then, in the 1990s, large numbers of refugees from what used to be known as Yugoslavia arrived, fleeing the conflict and devastating conditions of the area.

At the turn of the millennium, Australia has found people from all these countries continuing to come in – some legally, some not – but it is now also facing a fresh influx from Middle Eastern refugees, especially from Afghanistan. Smugglers are charging between US$1,000 and US$3,000 per person for the boat trip from Indonesia to Australia, and considerably more for the total passage from the Middle East or Pakistan.

As noted in the Introduction, most refugees heading for Australia first enter Malaysia, where they are taken to the south before making a short ferry crossing to the Indonesian island of Batam. From there it is not difficult to reach Jakarta and go on to the southern Indonesian islands of Bali, Flores or Lombok where they embark for Australia.

Established smuggling routes are known to exist in Amman and Bangkok too. These ports facilitate movements out of the Middle East and North Africa. Bangkok is known to be a major centre for the production of fraudulent documents. Kuala Lumpur and Jakarta are also important hubs for people-smuggling activities. The spate of boat arrivals has come from several departure points in Indonesia, including West Java, South Sulawesi, Kupang, Lombok, Bali, West Kalimantan and Sumbawa.

Broken down, the statistics make for interesting reading in detecting patterns of entry to Australia (they are all based on the Australian tax year, 1 July to 30 June). In 1998–99 more people arrived illegally by air than by sea – 2,106 air travellers compared with 921 people arriving on 42 boats, but this changed the following year as 2000–01 saw more people arrive illegally by sea – 1,508 air travellers compared with over 4,000 people arriving on 54 boats. The 1,508 people refused entry at Australia's airports represent a decrease of 11 per cent on the previous year.

Malaysia was the largest source country for people refused clearance at Australian airports in 2000–01 (142), an increase of 24.5 per cent on the previous year. The number from Iraq dramatically fell from 325 in 1998–99 and 157 in 1999–2000 to 37 in 2000–01. The other high source countries were South Korea (136), an increase of 25.9 per cent; New Zealand (111), an increase of 3.7 per cent; Thailand (100), an increase of 35.1 per cent; Indonesia (92), an increase of 70.3 per cent; and United Kingdom (81), an increase of 14 per cent.

But as noted, the number of unauthorised arrivals by sea has been where the most dramatic rise has been. In 1998–99, there were 42 unauthorised boat arrivals carrying 921 people. In 1999–2000, there were 75 unauthorised boat arrivals carrying 4,175 people. In the financial year to 30 June 2001, there were 54 unauthorised boat arrivals carrying over 4,000 people. The main groups have been from Iraq (1,009) and Afghanistan (2,270). Comparing 1998–99 to 2000–01, this is an increase of 349 per cent in people arriving by boat, even though only 12 more boats arrived.

People are identified as arriving illegally in Australia if they arrive with no travel documents, or present documentation that is found to be fraudulent. People who arrive in Australia without authority are required by law to be placed in immigration detention until their situation is resolved. These camps have been strongly criticised over the years.

In January 2002, at one of Australia's larger camps in Woomera, 300 miles north of Adelaide, more than 100 Afghanistani people including children sewed up their lips as a protest over delays in processing their visa applications. Prime Minister John Howard did nothing to help the debate when he said: 'Do you really imagine that if a eight- or ten-year-old child begins to sew his or her lips together that a responsible parent would do other than stop him or her? I'm not going to randomly brand people as child abusers. I don't think it's responsible of me to do that. But I do know this, that the children in the proper, positive care of their parents don't sew their lips together, do they?'

It was not the first bit of trouble for the camp. Just a month or so earlier, there were three nights of rioting, during which more than 300 detainees rampaged, setting fire to buildings and throwing stones at staff. More than A$800,000-worth of damage was caused and 21 staff were injured.

But the conditions at Australia's detention camps have been criticised for a long time. Many of the detainees say they have been held for years without a hint to the legal processes that are determining their fate. Conditions got so bad in one camp that in 2000, three Somalis who had been held for almost three years asked to be sent home rather than continue their stay. 'We could have expected such treatment from a Third World country in Africa', they wrote in a letter to immigration officials, 'but not Australia.'

One official government inspector called the camps 'unacceptably overcrowded' and condemned medical services as 'disgracefully inadequate'. He described dental treatment there as consisting of a dentist who visited once every five or six weeks, whose main task was to pull out teeth in makeshift facilities.

An independent inquiry report published in February 2000 included charges of detention staff humiliating and abusing inmates, and treating children like criminals, making them work as cleaners and gardeners in the centre for A$6 a day. The situation is so bad for so many people that attempted suicides by drinking disinfectant or shampoo, beating themselves with rocks and slashings are all on the rise in the camps.

John Howard has tried to build bridges with Afghanistan immigrants – who have been treated terribly post-September 11 – by suggesting to them that if they fled Afghanistan because of the Taliban, then they should consider going back now because the Taliban are no longer in power.

One of the measures the Australian Government has put in place to combat the millions of people trying to enter the country is increased penalties for Migration Act offences. For example, the crews of Indonesian vessels bringing illegal immigrants to Australia are now receiving prison sentences of around four years with a non-parole period of two years, compared to the sentences of three to six months given out previously.

Indonesia-based smugglers have responded to the increased penalties in various ways. One is by using escort vessels to remove as many crew members as possible before the transporting vessel enters Australian waters. Another is by using young male crew members who claim to be less than 18 years of age in the hope that they are dealt with as juveniles. They also attempt to 'dump and depart' where circumstances permit (that is, disembarking the illegal immigrants and returning to Indonesia). Other responses by Indonesia-based smugglers to law enforcement pressure include bringing their clients into Indonesia using new routes and methods and departing from different areas of the Indonesian archipelago.

And no matter what the law tries, there will always be people wanting to enter the country, including young women like Malki, originally from Iraq. Malki studied medicine abroad and when she returned home, she found it oppressive and yearned to leave again. 'I had got used to the more outspoken ways of the West where you had more of a free choice in things. You could go to the mosque when you wanted, you could refuse to join certain groups – something made very hard in Iraq, so I decided to leave and set about raising the US$5,000 so that I could go to Australia.'

That sum helped her to get a passport with a false name and photograph, which got her to Jordan, where she tried to find a smuggler to sell her a fake visa to go to Malaysia. She knew she could not linger in Jordan because tales are rife of Iraqis going to the United Nations in Jordan and asking for asylum, only for the alien to be taken to the Jordanian authorities and sent back to Iraq.

Malki ended up travelling to Kuala Lumpur and then on to Indonesia where she met a man who planned to put her on a boat. On the first trip, they set out in an open fishing boat for Christmas Island, but it began to take in water after a storm and they had to return. The second attempt was in a bigger ship, but its engines broke down during another storm.

She remembers: 'It was terrifying for the 300 or so of us who were on the boat. Many people were seasick and vomiting. They were being sick and praying. Many thought we would all die. Water was getting into the ship and we had to use buckets to bail it out for three nights. Some refugees were engineers and they managed to repair the engines and we turned back again.

'Many of us wondered if we should go back to Iraq, but that was impossible. I would be executed immediately so I waited for a third crossing opportunity. The third time we sailed to Ashmore Reef, and there were no storms. From there we were towed to Darwin and then sent to the detention camp at Derby.

'We spent the first month in tents. It was very hot and uncomfortable. Then we had *dongas* [basic makeshift accommodation], they were much better.'

Malki said that for the first month most people were very happy to be safe in Australia, but as time wore on they became depressed and discouraged. 'We were not treated with respect. I do not understand why authorities would want to humiliate us unless they were trying to provoke us to do something foolish. We had head counts at 2 am, 3 am and 4 am on the same night. We would be awakened and all counted.'

Malki was granted a three-year temporary visa and, since being interviewed in May 2002, has been receiving a special government benefit of A$680 fortnightly plus A$160 rent assistance for a flat that costs A$400 a fortnight. She is also trying to get back into the medical world and pick up the threads of her life.

Immigrants trying to sneak into Australia by boat have always been the most high-profile of illegal cases there, but the whole country was shocked in October 2001 when a group of Iraqi refugees appeared to be throwing themselves and their children into the Indian Ocean to die after being told they were not allowed asylum in Australia. There was further shock in the media when it was reported that the ramshackle boat had been fired upon by the Navy frigate HMAS *Adelaide*, which was part of the naval patrol that patrolled looking for asylum seekers trying to sneak in. The boat, laden with around 220 refugees, had been discovered by the *Adelaide* near Christmas Island.

What made the matter even more potent was that the country was in the middle of an election campaign, which was already dirty and sordid. Howard's Government wasted no time in making the most of the situation. Immigration Minister Philip Ruddock told reporters that some of the asylum seekers threw themselves and children overboard after naval officers had boarded the vessel and ordered it back into international waters. He said sailors had rescued the people and returned them to their vessel. John Howard described the incident as an attempt to 'morally blackmail' Australia.

Howard's tough stance drew unprecedented international criticism, but at home the Government's popularity soared only weeks from national elections.

However, then the Australian Broadcasting Corporation said that unidentified sources from the HMAS *Adelaide* had reported that the Navy fired shots across the bow of the refugee boat before sending armed sailors to board the vessel – at which stage the refugees jumped overboard. Ruddock admitted that the *Adelaide* had fired shots across the bow, but refused to confirm whether the boarding party was armed, and insisted his version of events was correct.

It was also later revealed that the Navy tried to set the record straight and there were allegations that the Government, who had claimed to have a video backing up their claims, tried to cover things up when they learned the video showed the opposite. What is known is that before the election, in front of the general electorate, the Government stuck to their general account of the immigrants jumping into the sea. Australian civil servants, including the top senior civil servant, Max Moore-Wilton, defended the original version of events too. Mr Moore-Wilton, the head of the Department of Prime Minister and Cabinet, told a Senate inquiry: 'I am not aware that children have not been thrown overboard. It has not been established that children were not thrown overboard.'

The matter became complicated further when it was revealed that the picture showing the children in the water was not an isolated image, but part of a set that had been withheld. That set showed that instead of the children actually being thrown into the water in protest and to force another boat to pick them up, they were in the water because their fishing boat had sunk. It was also revealed that the photographs were not taken during the confrontation with HMAS *Adelaide*, as the Government had earlier stated. They were actually taken the next day, when the asylum seekers were being rescued by the *Adelaide*'s crew.

Senate hearings and investigations revealed what appears to be the truth of the matter. While the Australian Navy are shown in an excellent light, the Howard Government is shown up as ready to use any situation to their advantage.

The drama started in the early afternoon of 6 October 2001 when, after receiving shore-based intelligence, the HMAS *Adelaide* and a Royal Australian Airforce aircraft intercepted a wooden-hulled vessel with 50 people visible on its deck. The 25-metre vessel was at this time about 100 nautical miles north of Christmas Island, well outside Australia's area of jurisdiction, but was heading south at about 8 knots, and it was believed that the boat was heading towards Christmas Island.

As per standard procedure, the crew of the *Adelaide* shouted a number of warnings and instructions, telling the boat to turn round and that it should not enter Australian waters as it had no permission to do so. The immigrants ignored the shouted warnings and showed aggression towards the *Adelaide* while continuing on their course for Christmas Island.

By the next morning, the boat had entered Australian waters and the order was given to *Adelaide* Commander Banks for warning shots to be fired. He recalled to a Senate hearing: '[The boat] was, at this stage, well inside the Australian contiguous zone, approximately 2 to 3 miles from the Australian territorial waters of Christmas Island, and proceeding directly towards Christmas Island at about 7 knots. I need to emphasise that only aimed shots were fired into the water, about 50 to 75 feet ahead of the vessel. A searchlight was used to illuminate both the weapon-firer and the area in the water ahead of the vessel where the rounds were to land. This ad hoc process was introduced by me to clearly show my intent.'

The warning shots – and continued loudspeaker hails – had no positive outcome and the decision was taken for the boat to act more aggressively towards the immigrant vessel in preparation for a boarding, which took place at 4.45 am. The group quickly seized control of the ship, dealing with the passengers, some of whom were angry, while others threatened to commit suicide, gesturing with wooden sticks. Fourteen people jumped into the sea but were rescued. At the same time, others were beginning to sabotage the vessel in an effort to force the issue and make the *Adelaide* crew take them to Australia.

Meanwhile, a second boarding party and medical teams came onto the boat but they weren't made welcome. For example, water that was being handed out as medical relief was being thrown overboard, and repairs that were being made to the boat were being undone the minute guards left them. But eventually the boat managed to get underway and it was steered towards Indonesia. The *Adelaide* parted company from the boat 24 miles from Christmas Island.

However, after surveying the condition of the boat and the imminent poor weather conditions, Commander Banks decided to track the boat while staying out of their line of sight. This proved a wise move, as just hours later the boat raised a white flag and other distress signs. The *Adelaide* returned to a more positive reception. A quick investigation revealed that there was water in the fuel, the starter motor was sabotaged and the diesel rocker cover had been removed.

The boat was then towed to Christmas Island to await further instructions from patrol headquarters. In the meantime, sailors from the *Adelaide* continued to pump water and, for a while, it looked as if the immigrant boat could be made seaworthy. Commander Banks at this point refused to let woman and children come off the boat, believing that if he did, he would have failed in his orders.

'If I disembarked some to the *Adelaide* I would have failed in my mission aim and I might as well have embarked all of them. In my judgment we still had a boat that was still marginally seaworthy and I still had control of the situation. Clearly, if the aim was always to deter their arrival in Australia, embarking them on the *Adelaide* was another step towards their achieving that goal and our being unable to reverse the process. It could have been that I was directed to tow them back to Indonesia and transfer control to Indonesia. Having embarked them in *Adelaide*, that would have been an impossibility.'

But later that night, still 16 nautical miles north-west of Christmas Island, the boat started to go down quickly and all the immigrants began to jump into the water. It was of this episode that the photographs were taken. The immigrants ended up being taken to Papua New Guinea to have their claims assessed. Subsequent hearings revealed that the

Navy had mistakenly reported that children had been involved in the earlier jump into the sea, and this is how the false story that the Government capitalised upon began.

The timing of the inquiry was very difficult, as it was happening just as the news of the people at Woomera detention centre sewing their lips together during their hunger strike was breaking. While that individual matter has been resolved, the larger issue has not. Australia at the start of the twenty-first century will continue to be one of the more controversial parts of asylum-seeking history in modern times.

4

OUT OF AFRICA

Africa is the cradle of the human race, the place from which our ancestors started to roam the Earth 7 million years ago and where its population continues to do so to this day. Of all the continents, it is perhaps easiest to understand why people are fleeing Africa. It is a continent of 50 nations and almost 700 million people and has been ravaged by droughts, famine and pestilence. It may have been the birthplace of humankind, but at times it also looks and feels like the death of humankind. There is misery on a massive scale because of a combination of greed by the rulers of individual countries, the impact of colonisation and poor international planning that includes the strict and even harmful economic policies requested by the WTO to ensure repayment, with interest, of loans.

So it is no surprise that a large number of people want to leave and find a better life for themselves. For such people, there are a number of options. The most popular one is getting to Morocco and from there to Spain. Another increasingly popular option – especially among the traffickers – is to go through Libya, which provides sea routes to Italy's coastline. But it is a perilous journey: at the end of November 2002, more than 50 immigrants perished when a fishing vessel ran into difficulties not long after setting sail.

However, not everyone wants to leave Africa completely. Of the estimated 8 million who have tried to leave parts of Africa over the last few years, at least 3 million migrated within the continent, mostly to South Africa.

Most illegal African migrants work in the informal sector of South Africa's economy as street peddlers or day labourers, and particularly in the gold and diamond mines where almost 200,000 people work. Territorial battles break out, and polls show that many South Africans are unhappy about immigration to their country. Immigrants are blamed for rising crime, unemployment and homelessness. In order to combat the problem, the South African Government started imposing US$1,000 fines for transport operators who brought anyone into the country without proper documentation.

It is not hard to see why South Africa is attractive. The per capita income is US$3,000, whereas in Mozambique, Malawi and Zaire, for instance, the per capita income is less than US$100. It is also more stable than other countries.

Zimbabwe has made the headlines more often than the rest because of the regime being run by President Mugabe and his party, Zanu-PF, who have dominated Zimbabwe's politics since independence in 1980. Over the last few years, militias have roamed the country, chasing out many white Zimbabweans and forcing them to hand over their land.

Mugabe won the 2002 presidential elections, but the result was considered seriously flawed by the opposition and foreign observers. Since then, conditions have deteriorated with the rule of law completely disappearing and militia attack by hundreds of Zanu-PF supporters being commonplace. The main opposition party, the Movement for Democratic Change (MDC), has to operate almost under subterfuge because members known publicly face beatings and death. Even worse is the fact that other governments are doing little to help. If they arrive in Britain, many people who manage to escape from Zimbabwe are just sent back.

One person this happened to, who would give his name only as Ken, told of the troubles he went through to escape his country, not once, but twice.

'I was leaving Zimbabwe because, like the rest of my family, I was a member of the MDC. My family were also of mixed race and that made things even more awkward. We were having stones thrown through the windows of our homes, cars vandalised and people being beaten up. We had had enough, so we managed to sell everything we had and send the cash to relatives in Canada.

'I ended up staying longer than most of my family as I was convinced things would improve, but eventually even I knew I had to go, so I decided to go to London and declare myself as a refugee. I got a flight over and, as soon as we touched down, I walked over to customs and declared myself an immigrant seeking asylum.'

Ken was placed in a detention centre – a converted army base near Bedford, where he was placed in a dorm with 20 other Zimbabweans, most of whom had middle-class professions, such as teaching, and were also members of the MDC. Ken did not like it there, finding it bleak and lonely, but at least it was safer than back home – or so he thought.

'It may no longer have been army barracks but it still seemed like an army life, as we were woken up at certain times and seemed to have no rights. Some people were taking sleeping pills. It was sad because these were people who wanted to be in Britain, who wanted to work, but were turning into zombies because of the slowness and humdrum nature of the process of being accepted. What made things even more bizarre was that we were entitled to things like sleeping tablets, but trying to make a phone call was hellish and difficult.'

But there was something more dangerous lurking there than bureaucracy and boredom – spies: 'I was warned by officials at the base that there had been cases in the past where people had infiltrated the base, posing as illegal immigrants, but it turned out that they worked for the CIO [Zimbabwean Intelligence Service] and, after they had been sent back home, they would tell their superiors who they had seen over in the UK. The spies pass information to the Zimbabwean Embassy and threaten dissidents with reprisals should they return home.'

What confused Ken was that he was also told by some fellow asylum seekers that the centre staff told everyone this in order to stop them all banding together and demanding better conditions. They pointed out that if no one trusted anyone else, then they wouldn't all work together to improve things, which would suit those running the camp.

According to the Refugee Council, several foreign intelligence agencies have infiltrated Britain's asylum system to hunt for dissidents who have escaped their grasp at home. Chief Executive of the Refugee Council, Nick Hardwick, said: 'It clearly happens. There will be people in the system who are working for their governments.'

However, there was one group that Ken and the others rarely socialised with – the ill. 'There was a room of people who we were told had serious diseases like AIDS. Apparently a lot of the people coming over did not know they had diseases until they were actually there and tested for everything. Once there, they were treated for the illnesses while their cases were being reviewed.'

Ken and others started to believe that it was better to come here ill than in good health. Under various international acts and conventions, the ill are hard to remove until they recover – for instance, under the Human Rights Act, patients who can show that they would not be able to receive the correct treatment for their condition back home are allowed to stay in a country that can treat them. So if someone arrives in Britain with HIV, for example, thousands of pounds are spent on their healthcare, just as the money would be spent on a NHS patient. Unofficial figures suggest that more than 2,000 immigrants have brought HIV into the UK – and immigration is now a larger cause for concern than either casual sex or homosexuality for the spread of HIV. Many countries have yet to release their figures for HIV-positive immigrants. In Britain the number has tripled over the past five years, and public health experts fear for the future but are afraid to speak up for reasons that are political – in more ways than one.

One public health worker told me: 'Zimbabwe and Nigeria are the two hotspots for HIV coming into Britain at the moment. Tanzanian cases are also on the rise. Speaking out about it causes those higher up the chain to fear that there will be even more reason for race riots if the truth of the situation got out. Politicians are running scared from this because it's a no-win for them. They are accused of being soft if they treat the people but hard-hearted if they throw them out right away.

'The biggest worry is that these are the cases we know of from the immigrants who come to us. How many others are there? It's a frightening thought but I – and many others – believe this is a time bomb that will go off. Immigration is the biggest threat with regards to HIV at the moment.'

Some people near Ken considered drastic steps. 'One person asked if a HIV person would inject him with blood, thinking it might improve his chances. Others tried to get blood from them – but not put it in their system – but that plan was flawed as doctors take fresh blood from people in front of them. They don't rely on stale blood.'

However, Ken kept his distance. 'I didn't want to fall ill or catch anything. If I'm being perfectly honest, I didn't want to be anywhere near them.'

Ken spent three months in the centre with only a few meetings to determine his situation; each time being told that he was being taken to another meeting. 'I welcomed the meetings,' he said, 'as they were a break from the boredom and paranoia. I also hoped that each meeting took me one step nearer to being away from the place and into freedom.'

One meeting was slightly different, though. He was taken to Gatwick Airport, handcuffed and put on a plane back to Zimbabwe. 'I was terrified. I had been taken there under the pretext that my asylum was going to be discussed but when we got there, I was taken into a room, handcuffed, told I had been unsuccessful and was being taken back home. I was stunned and couldn't believe it. They led me like a lamb onto the plane.

'The hostess told me that I wasn't the first person to be sent home like that. According to her it happened at least once a week. She said that the best thing to do was to put up a fight, kick and scream because then some flights would refuse to take you and perhaps even contact helpful agencies for you.'

Virgin Atlantic have done this in the past but according to a spokesperson there is no official line on the situation. The air steward's advice was no consolation for Ken as he was on his flight. 'I was convinced that I was flying home to die, my life was over. I knew the odds were that the passenger list was already known back home and the CIO would have seen it.

'So I wasn't surprised when I got there and was met by two officers who took me away. They told me that they would be taking me to a police station for a little chat before releasing me to my family. I told them I had no family. They then started saying that they would have to arrest me then for vagrancy and that if I had no relatives here, then no one would miss me if I disappeared. I was terrified.

'When we got to the police station, I was thrown into a room and they started hitting me on my legs and back with rubber sticks. One of them brought in a hose as well, and put my feet and face into buckets of ice. They said I was a traitor to the country, that I should be ashamed of myself and I should reveal who else I knew who was a traitor so that I could at least die with dignity.

'But I told them nothing. After a few hours they threw me out, telling me that they looked forward to picking me up as a vagrant. I was terrified again. I had been abandoned by the British and now I was being abandoned by the CIO – but I knew they wouldn't be leaving me alone for a long time. That was the terrifying part.'

Ken considered his options. The only thing he knew for sure was that he had to get out of Zimbabwe quickly. He had some money available – enough, he thought, to get him back to England ('I still hadn't actually heard if my family had made Canada or not, so I didn't want to go over there until I knew for sure.'). His first thought was for The Gambia. Relatively high salaries attract medical doctors, lawyers and accountants. However most Ghanaians, Nigerians, Guineans, Sierra Leoneans and Liberians in The

Gambia are teachers who planned to work there for a year or two and then use the country as a stepping stone to Europe or the USA, but were unable to get visas and remained there. Increased checks on the borders put Ken off this plan.

This left him with just a few options, all of which involved heading towards Spain. Kenya and Nigeria are the hubs for illegal movement out of Africa and Ken knew that if he could get to one of these countries he would have no difficulty in getting to the coast and then overseas. Two of the most popular spots for immigrants who can get to the African coast are the Spanish cities and former penal colonies Ceuta and Melilla, which are on the Mediterranean coast of Morocco. Since the mid-1990s, more than 8,000 people have entered each city every year, and thousands more are harboured in Moroccan cities such as Tangier and Tetouan while raising money to be smuggled across.

The sea between Africa and Spain is an excellent crossing point as the authorities rarely work together, thanks to a history of Spanish anger at the 'ineptitude' of African police forces and Moroccans refusing to recognise Spanish authority over Ceuta and Melilla. Morocco refuses to accept most non-Moroccan immigrants who are caught in Spain, even when the police believe they have used Morocco as a smuggling route. It is claimed by some that Moroccan police are complicit in the process and, with enough financial persuasion, will turn a blind eye when someone is trying to get past them or if they are handed back to them by Spanish police.

In an attempt to control immigration, Ceuta's and Melilla's populations of about 70,000 and 60,000 respectively were boosted with the growth of shanty areas for immigrants that have been sanctioned and acknowledged by the Spanish. This system hasn't been trouble free – the immigrants were moved after riots broke out when a group of Kurds were processed through the asylum system quicker and given better treatment than others. A new area on the outskirts of Ceuta houses 2,000 immigrants in cramped conditions. It is laid out by language and nationalities. A similar facility exists at Melilla.

Spain has special work and residence permits and many immigrants now obtain these and renew them on an annual basis. Some critics argue that this is not about the Spanish being humanitarian; it needs a workforce like every other country, especially to work in its rural areas as agricultural labourers – for example, in the Rioja vineyards, the orange groves of Valencia and the horticultural centres of Almeria and Murcia. Spain also faces the possibility of worker short-ages as it has the lowest birth rate in the European Union and is projected to see its population decline in 2010.

But just as there are now permits, so there are stricter punishments for those without them. Anyone without proper papers can be deported within 72 hours. Also, illegal immigrants who manage to avoid deportation are not allowed to join unions, receive home aid or schooling for their children or be able to demonstrate.

The last tactic employed by the Spanish is similar to the American model – they built a wall. Since 1998, Melilla's 6-mile border has been sealed by a pair of steel fences about 4 metres high, topped with sharp razor wire. Roads just inside the fences have been paved, so that patrols can easily travel the length of the border. The fences are equipped with halogen spotlights and noise- and movement-sensors, and video cameras and air-conditioned guard-towers line the fence at regular intervals. It has been harder to line the coast at Ceuta because of the rugged terrain, but illegal entry from there is more difficult than it used to be. All of this put Ken off this route as well.

Ken eventually realised that no matter what his route, it would be fraught with danger. Some people in his position had gone on other flights to the UK and tried to use that as proof of their desperation, but he was not confident it would be a wise option. He didn't want to be forcibly thrown back on a plane again. Instead, he was put in touch with a smuggler who promised to take him along what he called 'the scenic route', which meant via a trip to Spain's idyllic Canary Islands.

Compared to other smuggling prices it was not expensive – US$450 – but it was hazardous. More than 1,000 people a year die attempting to get to Spain this way. Ken's smuggler explained that it involved the double-edged sword of bribing the police to turn a blind eye to the boat coming in – thus the police would not patrol in the area, but if the boat hit trouble there would be no help around. The smuggler also warned Ken with a more callous tale, that some officers just leave a boat in trouble even when they are near enough to help.

Ken was to share a large, small-engined, rowing boat with a group of travellers from Laayoune, in the Western Sahara. They had travelled hundreds of miles to get this close to Spain and were not going to be denied now – they were less than 100 miles from freedom. What amazed him was how many pregnant women were making the journey. They set off late at night.

'The water was calm and the moon was out. The smuggler, who did not come with us, said we had nothing to worry about as police had been bribed. The journey was fine – cramped but bearable – for the first few hours, until people started to need the toilet. It wasn't a problem for most of the men but the women presented some problems and the boat at times threatened to tilt.'

The next problem was dehydration and some people started scooping up sea water to help – but of course this did the complete opposite.

'The journey took us almost a day and when we reached Lanzarote most people were just glad to be out of the boat. The man in charge of the boat gave some people mobile phones – apparently they had paid more and were also set up with places to go.'

Ken wasn't so lucky, in more ways than one. Unknown to him, it is common practice for the smugglers to call the authorities to have pregnant women picked up. While this might sound bizarre, the thinking is that they will get the best medical treatment from the authorities instead of perhaps suffering on the streets. So Ken found himself picked up by the police. Along with some others, he was taken to a centre at Las Palmas on Gran Canaria, where they were given food and clothing. He was starting to despair.

'All I had wanted was to be safe, yet I found myself being in more and more perilous situations – though at least I was still alive, which was not a guarantee if I had stayed at home. But all I wanted was a place to be myself. I was an educated man. I just wanted to live my life.'

Ken decided to try a new tactic. He managed to get in touch with his Canadian relatives and was delighted to learn that although they were still going through the immigration process, his family were safely there.

'It might sound ridiculous but in all my travelling, getting access to a phone was not the easiest thing. Most of the time, my concerns were staying alive and eating. It wasn't until I got to the Canary Islands that I actually felt safe in any way. All of Africa felt dangerous, though I know some of this is just paranoia from Zimbabwe.'

Ken – and his Canadian relatives – told the authorities that Ken would be flown over to Canada and the relatives would pay for a ticket. There was just one problem – a lack of a passport, but the authorities helped Ken on this one. 'When we got to the airport I was simply ushered through. They just wanted rid of me. If someone could pay for a ticket for me, then that was fantastic in their eyes. It would let them get rid of one more problem.'

The flight was uneventful. He and his family had concocted a number of schemes to make sure he got through at the other end. One was that he pretend to be another family member, one already living in Canada. Another was that he had lost his passport on the flight. If he had wanted to, he could even have gone to ask for asylum, but he was wary of this after what had happened the previous time. In the end, it didn't matter. He went through immigration without anyone asking him any questions and into the arms of his distant family.

Since then, some of Ken's family have been allowed to stay in Canada, others have been refused entry but are currently appealing. Ken is still an illegal alien, but he is hoping for some form of amnesty to be declared in the near future.

'The system is a mess,' he said. 'I have an education and don't mind paying my way in whatever society will have me. Yet I was thrown out of Britain when far worse people were allowed to stay in. It should not be that way.'

5

MANY COUNTRIES, ONE PROBLEM: TALES OF THE SEX SLAVES

When Sasha was younger she always wanted to see her name up in lights, to be a world famous dancer, entertaining thousands, watching their faces glow as she performed fantastic dance moves. And she has entertained thousands – but not in the way she expected. For Sasha became a sex slave, tricked from her native Ukraine and forced to live a degrading existence in squalid surroundings. At 24 she may only look a youthful 19, but she has grown up quickly over the last three years. She has witnessed men forcing themselves on women, women being beaten and girls as young as 14 shooting heroin into their eyes to numb the horror of their lives.

Over coffee in London, Sasha recalls how her life went terribly wrong. It all began back in the Ukraine when she wanted to be a ballet dancer. At first, her parents thought it was just a childhood fantasy, no more realistic than the average schoolboy's desire to become an astronaut. But she showed her parents that she was determined, passing up social opportunities to train solidly at home.

Her parents, impressed by her dedication, made a deal with Sasha. If she saved enough money, she could go to join the ballet. They weren't overly happy about her travelling on her own, but they could see that she wanted something different from them. She was destined for better than they had achieved and they were proud of that. Like every parent, they wished only the best for their child.

Then, on her twenty-first birthday, Sasha received the first of two surprises that would change her life forever. A friend passed on something she had seen in a magazine while on holiday in Turkey. It was a small advert looking for dancers in Belgium. A new school was to be set up, concentrating on women, and the school hoped that their pupils would become among the best in the world. Contact details were given and, after making a phone call, Sasha learned that she needed enough money to get herself to Moscow and US$1,000 for transport and initial accommodation, the rest of the travel arrangements would be taken care of. She would of course need more money for her equipment and to live on, and she could either take that with her or get a job in Belgium.

Sasha was a little worried by this. 'It was going to cost a lot of money and there was no guarantee of success at the end of it.' She started looking at her parents' life, thinking that perhaps it wasn't so bad after all – and if she didn't try when she had an opportunity then she couldn't be disappointed when she failed. She tearfully told her father this one night, and he replied that it was not about equipment, shoes or costumes. If she had heart and believed in what she was doing, then she would be a success. Her talent, he said, came from within, not from the clothes she was wearing.

For Sasha, this was a defining moment. 'Up until then, my father had never said much, but he told me that night that he was impressed by my conviction. His biggest worry was that I would be disappointed but he said I had to try. If I didn't, everything I had done up until then would have been a waste otherwise.'

Her father then dropped the second of the two surprises on her. If she truly wanted to go, then her parents would give her the money. They had some savings and other money (in the delight of the moment, she never thought to ask where it had come from) and she could have it to pursue her dream. 'When you are famous and rich, you can think of it as a loan,' her father joked.

Another call was made and she was told to make her way to Moscow and their representatives would be able to help her on the way from there. To Sasha, this confirmed that she was dealing with professionals. She pictured girls like herself being flown in from all over the world – from Paris, London, New York and Milan – all to be part of this glamorous, new dance troupe.

Three years on, the only dancing she was doing was to the tune of her pimp.

The journey had started well, after a tearful departure from her parents. Her father showed no emotion until the last moment, when he nearly squeezed the life out of her with a bear-like hug. Travelling to Moscow was uneventful, brightened by her dreams and hopes. 'At this stage, it was all just excitement. I kept looking about at other people and wondering if they were going to the same place as me.' But the dreams started to tarnish once she arrived in Moscow and handed over her money to an averagely dressed man, not a man who looked as though he was used to mixing in high circles. 'But I told myself that perhaps he was a just a driver and perhaps I had set my sights too high, expecting everything to be first-class treatment right away.'

She was put in a bus, which looked not unlike an American school bus, with about ten other girls. The journey was long, taking days. Sasha was concerned by the fact that they were staying in hostels, because surely a top establishment would have them staying in hotels? She could understand keeping costs down by not flying, but she was worried when she saw the quality of the places she was staying in. 'I consoled myself by saying that I was just being a snob and was thinking of the high life too quickly. The top hotels would come, I told myself, once I was a big star. My God, when I think back to how naïve I was, it is incredible! I justified that whole trip by thinking it was the bottom of the ladder and everyone starts somewhere before rising to glory.'

The other girls were still excited. Some of them were convinced that within a few years they would be conquering the world and, more importantly, places like Broadway, where they would have riches beyond belief and men fighting for them, a life so far away from the Russian grey of their parents.

It took over a fortnight for them to reach Brussels. All of the girls, by now a little jaded, perked up when they arrived at the city limits. However, they started to wonder what was happening when they were being driven into what appeared to be a run-down part of the famous city. They stopped in an area that, to Sasha, seemed even more derelict than some of the poorest parts of the country she had just left.

They were forced into a building and escorted to a dormitory where there were about 20 beds. Half of them looked as if they had been used recently. While Sasha and the others were wondering what was going on, one look at the girls already in the room should have made it quite clear what was happening. The girls were prostitutes.

'Has there been a mistake? Are we wrongly dressed?' asked one of the girls who had travelled with Sasha.

The girls in the room laughed, as did the men who had brought them here. Some of the girls turned round, as if to leave, only to find their way blocked by the men. One tried to shove through, only to be slapped back so hard that she fell to the ground.

'We were all terrified,' recalls Sasha. 'The men just left the room and said we had a night to get used to being there and that the girls would help us get used to our new lives.'

Slowly the horror sank in. Yes, they had been brought there to be prostitutes. Some of the women already in the room had been snared the same way, but others had taken to the streets by choice.

What Sasha was going through, while horrific, is sadly not unique. The latest figures estimate that, worldwide, up to 1 million women may have been taken or lured across the globe to be used as sex pawns for gangsters.

The UK has seen an enormous rise in this over the last few years, with the Home Office reports suggesting that up to 30,000 girls and women in the UK were forced to come from elsewhere and sell their bodies. More than 5,000 of these are young girls under 16.

But these figures pale in comparison with those in the USA. According to the CIA, there have been more than 50,000 females arriving in America for the last ten years. The vast majority of prostitutes in the country are not American. Western Europe, Australia and New Zealand also have their problems. While the latter two have brought in isolationist policies that make it harder, it is not impossible to get a woman into the country – it just costs more.

UN estimates suggest that up to 2 million women and children may be on the move at any time. Many girls like Sasha are leaving Thailand, Vietnam, China, Mexico,

Russia, the Czech Republic, the Philippines, Korea, Malaysia, Latvia, Hungary, Poland, Brazil and Honduras for the most part, enticed by false promises of a better life and then being forced to become sex slaves.

Not all leave home thinking they will be dancers. Some leave believing they are in love with a man who later sells them. Others are kidnapped. Some are orphans or runaways who are sold at an early age – this is particularly common in war-ravaged areas. And some don't even think that they are selling themselves by signing up with international dating agencies or internet dating agencies. Very few of these women, though, ever want to meet someone who works in Burger King: they mostly seem to want rich and fit men. Sasha's tale may involve Russia and Belgium, but it could be any two countries and cities from hundreds across the globe. At that moment, in a dark corner of Brussels, knowing that others were going through the same hell as Sasha would have been no consolation to her.

One of the older-looking girls told them that they would be staying there for only a few nights. After that they would sleep there only when there was no business. The way she said 'business' left Sasha and the others in no doubt as to what she meant.

Some of the girls started crying and the others – including the girls who had been already in the room – comforted them. As the night went on, it became clear that they were in serious trouble and there seemed to be little way of escaping because there was always one of the 'escorts', as the girls called the men, about.

One of the men came back into the room a few hours later with food from McDonald's. He told the girls that, yes, they were here to be prostitutes but that they could earn a good living from it and once they had earned the men over

$250,000 they would be free to do what they want. They could go home, travel or be like Annie – he pointed to the older girl who had been speaking earlier – and choose to stay on and earn money.

'I remember him telling us,' said Sasha, 'that it wasn't a bad life. As long as we didn't try anything foolish, we would be looked after and there would always be someone near to make sure that we were not in danger from any of the clients. As he left, he also told us that the girls already there – I remember he always referred to them as "ladies" – had ways of helping the girls get through any teething problems they might have. I wondered what he meant then. Of course now I know he meant drugs.'

That night was one of the longest in Sasha's life. She did not know what to think or what to do. All of the girls were terrified. 'We were too scared to try and escape. Also, a lot of us were weary – the travelling had been quite uncomfortable and it had been long days on bumpy roads and short nights in strange places. Many of us were exhausted. I think some were also in denial.'

The next day, some of the girls were kept in the room, while the others were taken to another part of the building. Sasha was one of the girls taken out of the room. When they came back they learned what had happened to the ones kept there – the men who were keeping them prisoner had raped them.

This happened to many of the girls over the next few days, with those who resisted being beaten up. It was then that the 'ladies' introduced the girls to large amounts of valium and other, stronger drugs.

Sasha remembers it all too well. 'They told us that they would help us cope. We weren't allowed to use alcohol because if we smelled of that, people might think that we were "booze hags". A lot of us took the valium before working and then some heroin afterwards. While you were under its effect, you really didn't care about anything. The problem was that when you were off it, you felt even worse about yourself because you were now on drugs as well. So you felt even more worthless, which played into the hands of the people who kept you.'

One thing that was always sure was that there was no way out. The occasional beating of one of the girls – but never on the face, legs or breasts – or raping helped ensure that. They were trapped. 'People ask me now, why we just didn't always try to escape and it sounds ridiculous but it's true. First, we were all young girls, countries away from home. We didn't speak the language, we had people watching over us constantly and they did wear you down.

'The drugs also numbed you – not just to the sex but to everything. You were alive but not living. Also, the men who were using you didn't really care about you – they didn't even really care about you being there. They just wanted to do their thing and leave. They would have had sex with anybody or anything. It was always just normal sex with things like oral sex and masturbation. That didn't make it any better, but it was just sex and you get numb to it. It's not easy but you just get used to it. You just lay on your front or back or stood up or did what they wanted you to. It was rarely perverted.'

Occasionally, one of the girls would try to escape, or there would be talk of getting help from the hundreds of politicians in the city, but the 'ladies' told the girls that while the parties that made up the European bodies were impor-tant, it was not in the way that they expected.

'Annie once told us: "Yes, they are very important. Many of them are among our best customers, travelling away from their wives often, living in hotel rooms," which some of the girls found to be true. They were no different from anyone else, throwing you aside like a rag when they were finished. They didn't care and some of the ones who claimed to, just said it to try and get your offers for free.'

Those associated with the EU are not the only ones to have found themselves accused of taking advantage of the very people they are meant to be protecting. Over the years, United Nations staff have tried to cover up various events and atrocities that have happened in their name. One UN worker was not going to stand by and let the men get away with it.

Kathryn Bolkovac worked with a UN International Police Task Force human rights team in Sarajevo in 1999 and slowly learned of a then-growing trade in young women from all over Eastern Europe who were threatened with death if they did not do as they were told. The women were also raped, starved and drugged to take away any resistance. What shocked her greatly was the discovery that UN personnel were involved.

As Head of the UN's High Commission for Human Rights (UNHCR) in Sarajevo Madeleine Rees noted: 'Some men, including Britons and Americans with wives and families back home, arrived expecting to have access to sex and when they landed in Bosnia, they seemed to abandon all the morals they had at home. UN workers and Nato soldiers know they will not be held responsible for their actions.'

Not all of the perpetrators in these countries are soldiers from armies. Among the UN workforce were 2,000 American police officers such as Kathryn operating for the International Police Task Force, many of whom were brought in by the US State Department through an agency, DynCorp. Kathryn reported what she'd found but instead of being praised for her efforts and work, she was demoted and later sacked. She was furious at her treatment and vowed to fight back, taking the International Police Task Force and DynCorp to court and an employment tribunal, which concluded that she had indeed been picked on by her superiors and sacked for daring to reveal what was really going on.

Another former UN member of staff David Lamb told the UK's *Mail on Sunday* in 2002 that the organisation was unwilling to get involved in sorting out the situation. He said: 'UN investigations failed to yield results or implicate international workers caught subscribing to it. Whenever involvement of UN personnel surfaced during investigations, support stopped.'

DynCorp has been investigated for other similar matters, including allegations of staff buying and selling women as prostitutes, but the claims have always been dealt with and settled outside of court.

Little of this mattered to Sasha, who ghost-walked through her life of sleeping with men and occasionally women, taking drugs and trying to stay compliant to avoid beatings. There may have been people elsewhere in the globe trying to help, but no one was helping Sasha. Not even Sasha herself.

Weeks moved on into months, birthdays came and went. Some of the girls were taken to work in the streets as well as in the buildings owned by the men. Sasha never wrote to her parents, not even a false letter pretending that all was well. And then one day, while she was out working, she was told that she would not be going back to the flat. She was given a case with clothes and an envelope. The envelope had a flight ticket and a passport. She was put into a car with a man called Michael, and she was told that she had been sold on. She would go live with Michael now – in London.

'The truth is that by this point I was more or less on drugs every day so it never even registered until I was in London what had actually happened. I was told that I now had to earn money to pay off my debt – which I had apparently run up by travelling with the supposed dance troupe and living in their property – for this man.'

She went through customs, posing as the wife of her new owner. Her drugged-up condition was explained as drug-related sickness, which was not too far from the truth. Her existence continued as before, performing sex acts on up to ten men a day, seven days a week, with her new owner also regularly expecting sex with her.

One difference was that a lot more of her work was on the streets, soliciting, having sex down lanes or in cars. She was never able to escape because one of Michael's colleagues would always have their eyes on the area being worked, collecting the money from the girls.

The biggest difference Sasha found was that in London more women were willing to pay for sex acts. While this initially repulsed her, after her cocktails of valium and heroin she didn't care. But it was one of these meetings that started to change her life for the better.

Sasha met with another girl, Marya, who was working for an anti-trafficking charity and posing as a potential customer so she could meet other immigrant women who had ended up as slaves. The 28-year-old's story of how she had ended up on the streets before escaping from prostitution was very similar to Sasha's.

Marya had worked as a dancer in Macedonia, but she was coerced into travelling to Italy where she had to sleep with up to ten men a night. Like Sasha, Marya used heroin as an escape. She was later moved to London, where she worked from 11 am to 6 am the next morning. Each girl in the dingy building had their own room and pretended to be masseuses. The months turned into years, until her 'boss' called one day to say he was running late and Marya took the opportunity to escape. She went straight to the police and over a number of hours she managed to communicate what had happened to her. The police put her in touch with refugee groups who helped her.

According to Sasha, Marya then went through what seemed like the ultimate slap in the face. 'Marya told me that she had tried to take Henry [her 'boss'] to trial, but was told there would be little chance of getting him prosecuted. The law, she was told, was very vague on sex-trafficking offences. In fact, their best chance for a prosecution was on the grounds of his living off immoral earnings, which usually carries a 2-year jail sentence.'

Marya was also warned that it would be her word against his and that she would face prejudice, not only from a male-orientated legal system but also because she was foreign and a drug user, and Henry – if they could even find him – did not appear to be.

'It also did not help that the building where she had worked now appeared to be empty. The police could tell what it had been used for in the past, but there was no sign of anyone there when they went. The theory was that Marya's bosses must have worked out what was happening and cleared out from it, setting up elsewhere. She felt so abandoned by this. Even the law wouldn't help her.'

While this left her feeling defeated, Marya was told to look at it as an opportunity. Other women who had escaped sent letters to the people they had stayed with, saying that they had run away and were staying away, but would go to the police only if their keepers tried to get in touch again. The women told Marya that such letters were normally sent from another part of the country – usually Ireland – so that the keeper believed the woman was far away.

The one thing that Marya did not understand was why the keepers did not pursue women who'd escaped. That was quite simple, she was told. It was easier to get another woman sent over than to go through the hassle of pursuit.

Marya left Sasha, telling her of a number of places she could go to for sanctuary. Sasha thanked her for her ideas. Marya pointed out that if someone had told her that she could get out, she wouldn't have believed her either, but there is more of a life out there. A better life.

According to Sasha, meeting Marya helped turn her around. 'Listening to her helped me in so many ways.' Her words were the first indication to Sasha that perhaps there could be more that just her current situation for the rest of her life.

Marya came back a few times after that, to try to meet others, but Sasha kept using up her time, prompting wise-cracks from Michael that perhaps she could become a 'women only' specialist.

Sasha was scared – terrified, in fact – but she couldn't get the thought of freedom out of her mind, being able to go home and see her parents, to be safe again. She begged Marya to help her escape, to come up with some plan that would get her out of there.

'After hearing her story, I wanted out. Knowing that there is someone there for you, perhaps even there to help you, makes such a difference. For the first time since I set off thinking I was going to be a dancer, I had hopes. The hardest part was trying not to show it, as that would have made people suspicious.'

Marya said there were a few ways of doing it. The best one was the most risky. Marya would continue to visit on a nightly basis, so that she looked like a regular client, and then one night they would drive off at high speed and try to get Sasha to a safe place.

The plan worked, though luck played an important part in it. One of Sasha's minders noticed the car moving off slowly and came after it. The car then accelerated to get away, running a red light that had a police car at the other end of the junction.

The police pulled them over and their presence deterred the minder from coming any closer. Marya and her driver explained what was happening and the police took them to a station, where they had to give full statements. After a couple of hours Sasha was placed in a safe home belonging to Eaves Housing for Women, which aims to offer safety to trafficked women.

The next couple of weeks were not easy. Coming off drugs was as terrifying, and she spent every moment expecting to be yanked back to the life on the streets, to sleep with scores of men on a weekly basis. That did not happen, but there was no happy ending for Sasha.

When she attempted to get back in touch with her parents, she was informed that they had died. Her parents had left things for her, but they had gone to their graves wondering what had become of their daughter. Although she had no one to return home to Sasha did go back to visit her home in the middle of 2002. She has come off the drugs fairly well but is terrified for her future. 'So many girls who have been through what I have, have heard of the gangsters finding them and getting revenge, which scares me, but that is not my biggest fear.

'I am terrified that I have thrown my life away and all I am good for now is being on the streets, being a prostitute. It scares me to think that a part of me knows that if times are tough financially I could do that and use drugs so that it did not affect me. I hate myself for thinking it, but that doesn't stop the thought being there.'

Sex slavery is not just a European problem, or a Western world problem, as 28-year-old Anita Sharma Bhattarai from Nepal told the United States House of Representatives Subcommittee on International Operations and Human Rights, on 14 September 1999.

'In 1998 my husband took another wife. Soon after that, he began to beat and torment me, and to disregard my children. I decided it would be best if I and my children moved out of our home so that I could support us.

'I made money by buying vegetables from farmers and selling them in the village market. On 22 November 1998 I boarded the bus to go to pay for my vegetables. I sat next to a Nepali man and woman. They offered me a banana to eat and I took it. Soon after I ate the banana, while I was still on the bus, I got a very bad headache. I told the man and woman that I had a headache and they offered me a pill and a bottle of mineral water to help me swallow the medicine. Immediately, I felt myself becoming groggy and then I fell unconscious.

'The next thing that I remember is waking up in the train station in Gorakhpur, India. I am from a Nepali mountain village. I did not know what a train was and, of course, I had never been to India. I asked the man where I was. I was confused by the long cars that I was riding in and the strange surroundings.

'The man told me not to cry out. He informed me that there were drugs (hashish) tied around my waist and that I had just smuggled them across an international border. He told me that if I attracted the attention of the police, I would be in trouble for smuggling the drugs. I did not remember the drugs being tied around my waist but I could feel plastic bags on my stomach under my dress.

'The man also told me that if I stayed with him, I would receive 20,000 rupees from the sale of the drugs when we arrived in Bombay. I did not know how to get back to Nepal, I do not speak any Indian languages, and I believed that I was already in trouble for carrying drugs. The man told me that he was my friend and that I could refer to him as my brother. I decided to stay with him. It was a 5-day journey to Bombay by train.

'When we got to Bombay, he told me to wait at the train station while he went to sell the drugs. When he returned, he told me that the police had confiscated his drugs and that he did not have any money. He said that I would have to go to his friend's house and wait while he got some money. He called his friend on the phone from the train station, and she came to meet us there. She was a Nepali woman. She said her name was Renu Lama. I left the train station with her. My "brother" told me that he would meet me at her house at 4 o'clock that afternoon.

'As I walked with Renu Lama, she told me not to look at people because she lived in a very dangerous neighbourhood and there were some bad people that I should not make eye contact with. When we arrived at her house, she told me to take a bath. I told her that I would wait until 4 pm when my "brother" came because he was carrying my clothes. She told me my "brother" was not coming. I waited until evening but he never came. Finally, I took a bath and Renu Lama gave me some of her old clothes to wear.

'Renu Lama then asked me if I could write a letter for her. I did. She dictated what she wanted to say to her family, and I wrote the letter. When I had finished writing, Renu Lama took away the ink pen. She went to my room and took away all of the pens, pencils, and paper that I could possibly write with. I realised that the writing of the letter had been a test. Now that they knew I was literate, they were keen to keep me from communicating with anyone outside.

'I felt very scared that evening and I refused to eat anything. I soon noticed that many men were coming in and out of the house and I realised that it was a brothel. I began howling and shouting. I said that I wanted to leave.

'Renu Lama told me that I was ignorant. She said that I had not come easily and I could not go easily. She said that I had been bought and I would have to work as a prostitute in order to pay them back. I was never told how much they had paid for me. Renu Lama and two of her associates told me that all the women in the house were "sisters" and that we had to support each other. I cried a lot, but they comforted me and brought me a fine dinner – complete with chutney and a pickle.

'The next day, though, I insisted that I wanted to leave. The women began to slap me on the face. They cut off my hair. It had been shoulder-length at the back with a short fringe at the front. Now that I had short hair I knew that I could not leave the brothel without everyone identifying me as a prostitute. In my culture, short hair is the sign of a wild woman.

'Then I was told that all the women in the brothel had to bathe three or four times each day. The women all bathed nude and together – four or five girls at a time. I had never bathed nude before, and never with other naked women. When I expressed my shyness, the other women mocked me. They grabbed me and stripped off my clothes. They forced me to bathe with them.

'For the next couple of days the women beat me often. They slapped me on the face and head with their hands and hit me about the waist and thighs with metal rods. I begged to be let go. I said that I wanted to return to my children in time for the biggest holiday of our culture. The women mocked me. They told me that if I worked with them for a couple of days, they would send me home with three bricks of gold and 30–40,000 rupees for the festival.

'I was also forced to learn Hindi – the language of most of the customers. When I couldn't speak enough Hindi, I was beaten about the waist and thighs with the iron rods.

'When I was alone with one of the other women, I offered her my gold earring if she would let me go. She said no. Later I learned that three of the women were in the brothel voluntarily and they were the owners and in charge. There were six other women in the brothel and, I learned, they had all been tricked and forced like me. Renu Lama and the woman to whom I had offered my earring were two of the brothel owners.

'All of the women in the brothel were from Nepal. The six who were forced had all been brought from Nepal but under different pretences. One girl had married a man who had said he was taking her to Bombay to buy gold. He then left her in a brothel.

'None of the other girls could read or write. I am literate because I am Brahmin and the women in my community are educated.

'The women tried to reassure me that being a prostitute was not that bad. All of my food, housing, and clothes were provided. All I would have to do, they said, was sell my body.

'On the fourth day that I was in the brothel, my first client came to me. I refused to have sex with him. He had already paid for me so he grabbed me and tried to rape me. I fought him off. He had managed to get my clothes off but he was very frustrated because I was resisting him so much. He stormed out and asked for his money back. A couple of the brothel owners came in and beat me. When they had finished, the same man came back in. I then said that I would have sex with him only if he wore a condom. I knew about the need for condoms since I had learned that some of the other victims had very bad diseases. At first he refused but after another fight he finally agreed to wear a condom. By the time he left, he had used three condoms.

'I had only one client on my first day. But the next day, and every day after, I had three or four clients. I managed to get an ink pen. I would write messages to the police on the inside of cigarette boxes and send them out with my clients. Many clients promised to help but none did.

'Each client paid 220 rupees to be with me for an hour. I had to give the entire sum to the brothel owners. Often, the men would give me five or ten rupees extra. I used the money to buy condoms since the brothel owners would not provide them for me. I was not able to go out to buy the condoms myself. In fact, for the entire month and a half that I was in the brothel, I was never allowed to go out into the sun. Some of the other girls went to the hospital when they fell ill. But I never got sick, so I could never leave.

'I lived on the second floor of the brothel. The six of us who had been brought there against our will were kept on the second floor. There were no windows on our floor. The three who ran the brothel lived downstairs, where there was a door that led outside. Several iron rods used for beatings leant against the wall beside the door. One of the owners always guarded that door. Outside it was a metal gate. When customers were not coming in and out, the gate was closed. The gate was held by a heavy chain that was locked by a large padlock.

'One night I tried to run away with one of my associates. We were caught by the brothel owners before we even made it to the gate. My friend was sold to another brothel in Sarat where the brothels are said to be even more immoral than the ones in Colaba, Bombay, where I was held.

'After serving clients for about eight days, an elderly man came to me as a client. When I was alone with him in the room, I told him that he was old enough to be my father. I told him, "I am like your daughter." I told him my story. He said that he had plenty of money and a Nepali friend. He promised to help me escape. He spent the entire night with me. That was the first time I had been with a client for more than an hour. I cried on him all night long. The next morning he left with a promise that he would send a Nepali friend to help me. He said that I would know his friend had come when a Nepali man came to the brothel, asking to be with Anita, and carrying a gift of sweets.

'A few days later, a young Nepali man came to see me. He brought a gift of sweets. I told him my story. He promised to help me escape. I told him that I did not trust anyone. In order for me to trust him, he would have to go to Nepal, report about me to my father and brother, and bring back some of my personal photographs as a result. The elderly client paid for him to go to Nepal. Before he left, the boy gave me his address in Bombay.

'Some of my associates overheard the owners saying that they were planning to sell me too to a brothel in Sarat because I was too much trouble. I decided that I could not wait until the boy returned from Nepal. I had to try again to run away. I asked some of the other girls to run with me, but they were too afraid. We had been told that we would be killed if we tried to run away. But I determined that I would rather die than stay in the brothel. The other girls pooled their money together and came up with 200 rupees. In exchange for the 200 rupees, I promised that if I made it out alive, I would get help for them.

'A couple of days later, I had a perfect opportunity. Renu Lama was out of town again. The owner who was watching the gate was drunk. A new maid had just been hired to clean and cook in the brothel. The new maid was doing chores and had left the gate open just a little. In the middle of the night – I would guess about 4 am – I ran out of the brothel. I was wearing only my nightgown and carrying a slip in my hand. I just ran down the street as fast as I could.

'As I was running, I saw two police officers. They were in civilian clothes but I knew they were police officers by the belts that they were wearing. I ran to them, told them my story, and handed them the address of the Nepali boy. They took 100 rupees from me in order to pay for a taxi. They put me in a taxi that took me to the Nepali boy's house.

'When I arrived at the house, the Nepali boy was not there. But another Nepali man and his wife were there. They were friends of the Nepali boy and they agreed to take me in. The police left me with that family.

'I did not know it at that time, but that same day, the Nepali boy had met Robert Mosier, Director of Investigations at the International Justice Mission. He told Bob my story. Soon after I ran away from the brothel, Bob and the police raided the brothel where I had been. After searching through the brothel, the police with Bob learned that I had run away earlier that night. They came with Bob and met me at the house where I was staying.

'Bob told me that I could go back to the brothel to get my things. I was too scared to go back because I thought I might be forced to be a prostitute again. But Bob assured me that I was safe. I went back to the brothel with Bob. I showed him all the hiding places where they found the other girls. All the girls who had been forced to be there were released from the brothel and a way was provided for them to go back home. The two owners who were there that night are now in jail. Bob also arranged for me to return home to my family in Nepal.

'First, I went home to my family but it was very uncomfortable. The people in the village laughed at me. In my culture, a woman is scorned if she is missing for just one night. I had been missing for two months. It was very hard for my family, especially since we are members of the Brahmin caste. So today I live in Kathmandu. I work as a domestic servant in the city. I am still without my children since they went to live with their father when I was taken away. I am told that my husband's new wife is very cruel to my children. But my husband does not want my children to be with me because of where I have been.'

According to Nepali welfare agencies, there are more than 200,000 Nepali women and girls in Indian cities with one fifth of them younger than 16. One survey showed that 5,000 Nepali girls are taken to India every year, many sold by poor husbands, relatives and even parents. But very few in the Western world hear of the plight of Indian and Nepalese women and girls. And worldwide, thousands stand on city streets like Sasha used to, hoping for a saviour, more likely to meet a rapist.

6

EUROPE: TERMINUS OF THE WORLD

'If I could have fallen in love with an English woman,' jokes Hallil, 'or if I hadn't been born where I was born, my life would have been a lot easier.'

Hallil is 36 and he has seen more of the world than most. He has also lived a far harder life than most. He has lived in Iraq, Turkey, Germany, Afghanistan and England. None of these countries have been particularly pleasant to him, but he is weary and wishes to stop travelling. He would like to settle, if only a country would give him the chance. Hallil's luck was against him from the moment he was born, because he is a Kurd.

As most people know, the Kurds are a large and distinct ethnic group in the Middle East numbering some 25–30 million people. The area that they inhabit – referred to on maps for centuries as 'Kurdistan' – spans modern-day Iran, Iraq, Syria and Turkey.

Hallil was brought up in the Kerkuk region of Iraq, in a village 81 miles north of Baghdad. From school he went to Mousul University, where he obtained a degree in sciences, and then spent a short time working in a hospital laboratory. But soon after graduating he was conscripted into the military. Although his father served six years in the Iraqi army, fighting the war with Iran, Hallil dreaded the prospect of joining up. The persecution of Iraqi Kurds under the rule of

Saddam Hussein is well documented and he was terrified that he would be forced to turn on his own people.

There were two options available to him. One was suicide, he took the other – he ran away. But running away meant he had to flee the country, as deserters from the army face execution.

Along with others, he paid US$6,000 to be smuggled into Turkey by hiding in a secret compartment in a petrol delivery tanker. He meant to spend just a few weeks in the Kurdish parts of Turkey, but he managed to bribe himself a new identity and stayed on, becoming active in the political process by such low key activities as attending meetings and distributing pamphlets – something frowned on by the Turkish authorities.

Half of the world's Kurds reside in Turkey, where they comprise over 20 per cent of the Turkish population. But they are an unwelcome fifth. When modern Turkey was founded, the constitution said that there could be no distinct cultural subgroups, which meant that any expression by the Kurds or other minorities in Turkey of unique ethnic identity was harshly repressed. For example, until 1991 the use of the Kurdish language, although widespread, was illegal. To this day, any talk that hints of Kurdish nationalism is deemed separatism and grounds for imprisonment, as many Kurds have discovered over the years.

Hallil knew of the possibility of imprisonment. He had seen it happen to his friends and one day, after two years in Turkey, Hallil was imprisoned for a week.

'I was tortured and left in no doubt one night that I had been marked as a troublemaker and potential terrorist. I had to get out.'

The very next day he took a bus ride across country to Istanbul, where he met a fellow Kurd ('a friend of someone whom I had met in my time there'), who fixed up the next leg of his trip. Hallil and several others were loaded into a lorry, where they were surrounded by crates to hide them from immigration officials. The lorry then boarded a ferry. The aliens were free to walk around the lower deck of the ferry during their six days at sea, but they couldn't go any further for fear of being discovered.

Finally the ferry docked somewhere in Italy and, still hiding amid the crates, Hallil was sneaked through immigration control. Then he was fixed up with a minibus ride which, after a long drive, delivered him to Paris, where he was left to his own devices.

Western Europe is a popular destination because the borders are so relaxed and the lifestyle seems better than elsewhere. In Paris, Hallil had a choice to make. 'I was given the option of going to Germany or Britain or elsewhere in Europe.'

Every European country has its own way of dealing with the many would-be immigrants it sees – in fact, they can't even agree on what defines an immigrant. For example, in Britain, an asylum seeker is anyone arriving in the UK who claims to show 'a well-founded fear of persecution because of race, religion, nationality or membership of a particular social group or political opinion', also the UN definition of a refugee. In 2001 there were 71,700 principal applicants (which rises to 88,300 when including dependent women and children). Figures show that 25,500 applied for asylum at port and 46,200 entered the country illegally, or as a student or visitor, and then decided to claim asylum. (You will notice that most figures quoted are for 2001, as official statistics can take over a year to compile.)

In any one year, decisions are still being made on applications from previous years. In total in 2001, decisions were made on 118,195 applications. Just under 11,000 of them were granted asylum or 'refugee status', 20,000 were given exceptional leave to remain, 87,725 were refused asylum and 9,285 were removed from the country. Of the refusals, more than 55,000 were appealing against it. A breakdown of the main countries from which applicants to the UK came in 2001 reveals that most come from beyond Europe: Afghanistan 91,901, Iraq 6,805, Somalia 6,500, Sri Lanka 5,545 and Turkey 3,740.

Meanwhile in Germany, the rules are much more gener-ous than the Geneva Convention's criteria. Asylum is given to refugees who flee their countries for political reasons, according to the Geneva Convention on Human Rights. A second group is allowed because they would face political persecution if they returned to their home countries. A third group is allowed on humanitarian grounds. In 2001, German authorities received 88,287 applications (12.4 per cent more than the previous year); 5,716 applications were accepted for political reasons, 17,003 for political persecu-tion and 3,383 on humanitarian grounds. According to official figures, 55,402 asylum seekers were refused asylum. In 2001, 5,566 asylum seekers came from Iraq, followed by Turkey and the Federal Republic of Yugoslavia.

France received 47,291 asylum requests in the same year, accepting 18 per cent of them on the basis that they fulfilled the terms of the Geneva Convention. The biggest group of asylum seekers were from Turkey, mostly from Turkish Kurdistan, with 5,347 claims, followed by 3,781 claims from the Democratic Republic of Congo, then 2,948 requests from China, 2,940 claims from Mali, 2,933 from Algeria, and over 2,713 from Haiti, Mauritania and Sri Lanka. In France, claims take between four months and four years to process. During that period, claimants have no right to work and they receive welfare benefit of about £200 a month for a maximum of 12 months

In Italy, the Italian Interior Ministry says that in 2002 there were 10,000 requests for asylum, of which 3,000 have been accepted. The ministry says there is no major problem with unofficial arrivals, although many politicians contest this (mostly those on the right wing).

In Spain, the term 'asylum' is rarely heard, although there is growing concern about immigration. There are roughly 1 million legal immigrants, about half from the EU and the rest largely from Morocco, Latin America and Eastern Europe, and an estimated 150,000 illegals. Many Africans fleeing the sub-Sahara are also held in Spain's African enclaves of Ceuta and Melilla (see chapter 4). In 2001, 13,000 illegal immigrants were deported while, in one of the Spanish Government's periodic amnesties, 120,000 had their status regularised.

Denmark is one country that immigrants try to avoid. In 2002, the Danish Parliament passed new legislation to tighten controls on immigration, including a bill that abolished the concept of de facto refugees (where anyone could claim to be a refugee and get help), allowing only individual asylum seekers and refugees entitled to protection under international law to live in Denmark. According to the state-run Danish Immigration Service, a total of 12,512 asylum seekers came to Denmark in 2001, mainly from Iraq, Afghanistan, Bosnia and Yugoslavia, with 53 per cent of them being granted asylum.

Why do would-be immigrants choose to try to enter Europe? According to a European Union report on forced migration published in 2002, most asylum seekers are driven there because of war and repression, rather than simply to seek greater wealth. The report for the Director-General for Justice and Home Affairs at the European Commission concludes that 'push factors' such as war and the repression of minorities far outweigh 'pull factors', such as economic hardship or Europe's benefit systems.

Significantly, the report also shows that the poorest countries of the Third World bear the brunt of immigration. The number of asylum seekers coming to European countries is relatively small compared with millions fleeing to countries such as Pakistan (2 million refugees in 2000) and Iran (1.9 million), or countries in or close to war zones such as the Federal Republic of Yugoslavia (484,000) or Tanzania (680,000).

Researchers from the Refugee Studies Centre at Oxford University examined the ten countries most refugees to Europe were fleeing. Seven had experienced war in the decade up to 2000 and the other three – Iran, Turkey and Romania – have a history of repressing minorities. Closer analysis showed that most Romanian refugees come from the country's suppressed Roma Gypsy population, and many of the Turks and Iraqis were in fact Kurds fleeing persecution. Many Iranians coming to Europe are from the minority Sunni population.

Hallil – a stranger in a strange land with no family in other countries – ended up making a logical choice on where to go. 'I chose Germany because I knew it had more Kurds and Turks there. I believed I would be safer and happier. I bore no ill-will towards Turks. I knew not all of them were like the ones in the police.'

Germany is one of the most popular spots for Kurdish and Turkish immigrants, with more than 600,000 living in the country. Part of its appeal is that Germany offers recognised refugees better conditions than neighbouring countries.

It was not easy for Hallil to settle. Although he managed to find labouring work and a summer job as a coastguard, he was attacked a number of times, both by Germans and Turks.

'People say Germany is a very European country, a passionate country where many different cultures and people meet, and that is true. Unfortunately, it is not always peaceful.'

He spent three years there before events conspired to move him again. In the interim he had begun a relationship with another immigrant, Ara, from Afghanistan. He had also found himself becoming political again, joining the Federation of Kurdish Associations in Germany, an umbrella organisation that brought together the Kurdish associations that work closely with the PKK. Even after it was banned in Germany in 1993 he continued to have ties to the group, and yet he was allowed to continue working in the country. Although he was not a citizen, he felt relatively safe – despite the occasional scrap with other nationalities – until July 1999.

Hallil was woken one morning to be told that a member of the PKK – who had been outside of Turkey and believed he had the protection of Germany behind him – had been kidnapped. Cevat Soysal, a supposed high-ranking member of the PKK, was abducted when travelling in Moldova and taken to Turkey by the Turkish Secret Service in July 1999. What scared many immigrants – especially those in Germany – was that Soysal was travelling on a travel document under the 1951 UN Convention Relating to the Status of Refugees. When political level enquiries were made about the removal of Soysal, the Turkish authorities reminded the world that under the 1951 convention, this travel document did not give Soysal any right to expect the diplomatic protection of the German Government, nor did it give them any right to exert such diplomatic protection on him if they wished to do so. The Turks reminded other nations that according to the convention a state has a duty to re-admit a refugee to whom they have issued a travel document, and that is all. A refugee does not receive the full diplomatic protection of the state.

The Moldovans were reluctant to get involved in the matter, even after Amnesty International pointed out that Moldova had a clear duty under international law not to expel, forcibly return or extradite a person to another state where there are substantial grounds for believing that he would be in danger of being subjected to torture. This legal obligation is part of the Convention against Torture and Other Cruel, Inhuman or Degrading Treatment or Punishment (CAT), to which Moldova is a party.

The German Minister of Foreign Affairs wrote to his Turkish counterpart to express concern about Soysal's alleged torture and health situation. Despite such letters, the fact remained that Soysal had been removed illegally from a country because of his political beliefs, and that terrified others who shared those beliefs.

Such events did not inspire Hallil to feel safe. 'Looking back, we were all probably scaring each other, saying that we could be next, and having self-inflated ideas of grandeur, but I was more scared than most as I was afraid of my full past coming out, so I knew I had to flee.'

Ara came up with the idea of going to Afghanistan. She knew people who could smuggle them back in as long as they didn't mind taking a few things in with them – notably guns. According to Ara, 'People rarely want to be smuggled into Afghanistan, it's more often guns, so we did not think it would be too much of a problem, especially as there are a lot of smuggling routes for people to get out through and the same routes are often used for other things.

'We didn't have a lot of money left so we wanted to do this as cheaply as possible. That meant we had to help people take goods into the country. We weren't happy about it, but Hallil wanted to get out of Germany quickly so it seemed to be the best option.'

The route was long – going via Pakistan – and fraught with danger. The authorities may not have been interested in people travelling into Afghanistan but the weapons many were carrying would be of great interest, and the penalty for carrying them high.

Fortunately, the couple were not caught and went to live with Ara's family at the start of 2000. Both of Ara's parents passed away during that year but the couple were still content living in the country, despite the Taliban regime, until 11 September 2001. 'Everything changed after that day. While not everyone knew who was behind it, there were enough people with suspicions.'

Hallil's sense of self-preservation took over again. 'It wasn't a case of thinking that Afghanistan was going to be bombed, but when reports started coming in that the suspects were from the Middle East, you knew this was not going to be a safe area. We decided that it was time to move again. Our main concern was whether we would be alive long enough to move. Many people expected to be bombed within days.'

The couple sold everything they had and got in touch with the smugglers. Unsurprisingly they were not the only ones and, that being so, prices started to rocket. Flights were out of the question as Hallil had no passport and they couldn't afford fakes, so they would have to face a long, tortuous route over land.

They were given a number of options. Ara remembers: 'We were told that London was US$16,000 by air, US$9–10,000 by land. Denmark cost around the same. Germany was US$14,000 by air but a lot less by land, though Hallil wouldn't return there.'

The couple left Afghanistan, being led into Pakistan by land, going south through Quetta and then turning west into Iran. 'We got through Iran without too much trouble,' said Ara. 'The smuggler told us to get off the bus at certain points. We had no papers to go into Iran. We had to sneak over the mountains. It took a couple of weeks to get through Iran to Tabriz near the Turkish border and then we had to wait around for the next smuggler to take us through the Ararat mountain range.'

The group had to be very careful and were told when walking to follow an exact route. The reason for this was very simple – land mines. According to Hallil: 'A smuggler told me that the authorities have marked the border with rocks and mines and that he would know the way only by the fact that he would have a message saying such-and-such a rock area was clear for the moment.

'We had been in Tabriz for 15 days, waiting for the smugglers to pass us on to the next person who would take us over the mountains into Turkey. We took water and some dates. It was snowing and very, very cold. After some hours wolves attacked us. We saw them in the distance coming across a plateau. There were five of them. The shepherds with us had sticks and they started to beat them and they ran off.'

While land mines are safe if you know where to stand – or where not to stand – and wolves can be chased off, there were other risks for Hallil and Ara, such as soldiers shooting at them. 'We were told that we would go across only when the conditions were too bad for the soldiers to stay on the mountain, which was reassuring in one sense but bad in another as people have injured themselves jumping down the hill on the Iranian side. There's a steep bit, with lots of ice and rocks there that they have to cross.

'Anyway, we tried to get across. We were walking all night and were crossing when the soldiers started firing at us. The two smugglers who were with us ran away. We were freezing and had no food so we tried to make our way down. Two shepherds found us and sold us on to another smuggler who put us in a truck that was going to Istanbul.'

By the time Hallil and Ara made it to Istanbul, crossing the 840 miles from the border to city, their original exit method – an oil tanker that also held people – had gone, but the smugglers promised to get them out another way: by sea. The couple went from Istanbul to Italy on illegal fishing boats run by groups known as the Albanian *scafisti*. This was very dangerous but Hallil felt they had no choice.

'You hear tales of them dumping bodies overboard if the Italian police or coastguard are near them. Their priority is their boat and not being caught, nothing else. But I felt that we had to, as I was desperate to get out of the area.

'It was terrifying. We were all huddled together under a tarpaulin on a large motor boat that was perhaps the size of a bus. A couple of times the engine stopped and we were warned not to move or speak or we would be caught.

'A couple of people were sick; some tried to hold it in, others let it out but quietly. No one told the *scafisti* because you did not know what their response would be. They could throw you off into the dark water if they thought you could be a problem.'

Once they reached Italy, they were put on a train to Rome and given the contact details of a man who helped Afghans and would get them on the way to the UK. That man put them in touch with another smuggler, who showed them how to sneak into a wholesale depot where trucks were leaving for the UK.

'We were put under washing-powder boxes. No one searched us or anything, but we had been warned: "Don't move, don't shake, don't talk – otherwise you will be found." We were given supplies but it wasn't very comfortable and there were a few embarrassing moments. Thankfully it was just the two of us.

'We were able to get out and move a bit at nights when the driver was sleeping, but only one at a time so the other one could stay hidden. Compared to some of the journeys though it was very comfortable and risk-free. At least no one was shooting at us.'

The only thing that kept the couple going was a scrap of paper with a phone number on it. They were told to call it if they reached England.

'After days, we reached England. We were exhausted but after the checks at the entry to England we jumped out and nearly terrified the driver. He threatened to call the police but we begged him not to. I lied that Ara was pregnant and we had been escaping an abusive family. He seemed to believe it.

'He asked if we had anywhere to go. I told him I only had a number to dial. He gave me some money to dial it because he said he wasn't going to let me use his mobile phone. The number was for a refugee help centre based near Kent. The driver said that as it was on his way, he would take us near it. He also gave us some food, which tasted fantastic. It was only a couple of sandwiches but it was our first real food in days as we had been living on biscuits and water.'

For a few moments, the couple feared that they were going to be taken to the local police station but the driver was as good as his word, dropping them off just outside Kent. From there they called the centre again and someone came and picked them up. That was in late October 2001.

Hallil and Ara were put in temporary accommodation. They now receive just under £40 a week each to help them get by. They are eligible for medical treatment and have recently been told that they can look for work, which they want to do. Because of the backlog in processing enquiries, though, they have been told that no final decision on their application for asylum should be expected until near the end of 2003. They continue to await news of their fate, which has now been complicated by them having a child.

Ara is pleased they have reached England, and hopes their journeys are at an end. 'I like Britain,' she said. 'I have found a country that I like – apart from the weather, a little – and I could stay here all my life.

'We do not know what will happen, though, and we have even been asked by immigration officers what we would do if one of us was allowed to stay and the other was told to leave. All we can do is hope.'

Hope may not be enough, as 2003 may see Afghans taken back to their homeland by force if they do not accept other reasons or inducements to go back home. The plan is part of a European Union clampdown on illegal immigration endorsed by EU leaders after electoral gains by anti-immigration parties in several member countries. The Danish Immigration Minister, Bertel Haarder, said the returns would be mainly on a voluntary basis, but added that the ministers had endorsed the use of force. He said the EU aimed to start the programme by April 2003, and would return about 1,500 Afghans a month. Diplomats have said that, according to conservative estimates, some 100,000 Afghans would be affected by the plan.

At the end of April 2003, the UK Government started its policy of sending Afghans home – even if they did not want to. Groups hit out at this with Margaret Lally of the Refugee Council saying: 'It is far too early for forced returns to Afghanistan when there is very credible evidence that the country is not yet safe and there is a climate of impunity and people's protection cannot be guaranteed.

'The structures of law and order and security are still being built up and, consequently, returning people at this time will actually worsen the situation.'

Ara was not amongst the first ones to go, but it may only be a matter of time.

Asmail would have liked to have spent his whole life in Turkey, but events conspired against him. He has lived in the UK for more than ten years and speaks better English than many of its native sons and daughters. When I met with him in London he was nothing less than a complete gentleman; the same could not be said of those around him. When he remarked, 'It's getting cold, even for a February,' a young man next to us – with a group of friends of course, not on his own – said: 'Well, fuck off back to your own country!'

Asmail was able to shrug the incident off with a sad and weary smile. 'When I came to Britain, I was told to talk about the weather as it is a very British thing to do and would help me blend in, but look at the reaction I get. I have a British passport like you, but I don't see them telling you to fuck off because you are Scottish.'

It may have been cold on that February day but Asmail preferred that to the treatment he had been getting in 1988, back in his hometown of Maras, in southern Turkey. For more than five years he had been a member of the outlawed-in-Turkey ERNK (National Liberation Front of Kurdistan), and had been arrested, along with a number of friends, several times in what he called 'a continued and consistent programme of persecution' by the Turkish authorities.

'They would suspend me by the hands from the ceiling of the cell for days at a time and they would beat me, hose me, give me electric shocks. One of their favourite tortures was the thing they call *falaka*, beating the soles of the feet with sticks. After that, the torturers used electricity – first to my fingers, then on the tip of my tongue, and finally to my genitals. I never told them much information, but I also knew that I could not last forever and I had to get out, so I did.

'It was arranged for my wife and children to stay with relatives, which was bad – especially as my wife was pregnant – but there was no other way to do it. It had been hard enough to get me moved and I was also worried about moving a pregnant woman.'

Asmail's friends in the organisation found an agent to arrange the illegal journey and, after a few people had contributed money, he paid the equivalent of about £2,000 and made all the travel arrangements. The original plan had been that he would fly in two steps to the UK, but he flew only as far as Italy. After that he had to travel by road but, as he said, 'It wasn't that bad. There were only five of us in a car, so while it was a little cramped, it was nothing like the conditions you hear of now. And even if it had been that bad, it would still have been better than the torture.'

Within minutes of arrival in the UK, Asmail went up to a police officer and told him that he was an illegal immigrant seeking asylum as he was being tortured back home. Bizarrely enough, the policeman did not believe him and Asmail actually found that he had to strike the police officer before he could get taken to a jail to plead for experts.

After a couple of few days, Asmail was put in touch with the Medical Foundation, a London-based charity that cares for victims of torture. Its doctors confirmed that Asmail had injuries consistent with numerous beatings. From there, it was decreed that he would be allowed to stay, but it took him two years to be given a permit to work, something he found very frustrating.

'I know people here, some like to not work, but I wanted to work. I wanted to prove that I could stay here, give something back and also earn money for my family and to bring them over here. It was a very slow process all the way through, right up until I received a British passport after ten years of being here. And I do not think that when I came here there were many people trying to get in like there are now, so it must be even worse nowadays. My family are going through the process, which seems different from what I went through, but it is still slow.'

Asmail started off with jobs that many would find beneath them, but he kept going and after five years he was given full refugee status. It took another three for him to be told that UK citizenship had been granted. At that point, he went out and arranged to use his money to take out a loan to buy a small grocery shop. He has also managed to bring his family over, sending for them years ago once he was able to work and provide for them. Money may not be in great abundance, but he has a home, he has his family and he is able to relax without people kicking his door in.

'I don't mean to make fun of this country,' he confides, 'but when I hear about people complaining that someone has shouted at them and called them a "Paki bastard" or something and that it's really distressed them, I find it hard not to laugh. Yes, it must be terrifying, but let me reassure you that it's nothing compared to being beaten up by officials. If the worst I had had back then was name-calling, I would never have left.'

And the general population of Britain would have been worse off if Asmail and others like him had not come here. While many right-wingers may find it hard to believe, Britain is better off financially for having immigrants, just as other countries are. A Home Office report in March 2003 found that legal immigrants to Britain made a net contribution to the economy of £2.4 billion – equivalent to 1p off the basic rate of income tax for every person who pays the tax. The report showed that immigrants cost Britain £28.8 billion in welfare claims and public services such as education, health, housing, transport and police in 1999–2000, but during the same period they contributed £31.2 billion in taxes. And while critics said that the report was flawed because it did not count illegal immigrants, the statistics are still worthwhile in helping to show the effect of the move of population into the UK.

The study showed that about 67 per cent of the British-born population were employed, compared with 55 per cent of immigrants. While 21 per cent of people born in the UK were registered as economically inactive, the figure for migrants was 30 per cent. Nonetheless, migrants received 12 per cent more in wage income and this was put down to many immigrants having highly-skilled occupations such as medicine.

Even the United Nations Secretary-General, Kofi Annan, said that immigrants were useful and a boon to other countries. Speaking on International Migrants Day, on 18 December 2002, Annan said: 'Immigrants and refugees should not – and must not – be seen as a burden. Those who risk their lives and those of their families are often those with the greatest ambition to make a better life for themselves, and they are willing to work for it.

'They do not leave their familiar surroundings, their culture or their families for a life of dependence, crime or discrimination thousands of kilometres away. They merely want a safer, more prosperous future for their children. If they are given a chance to make the most of their abilities, on an equal basis, the vast majority of them do.'

These are people like Emad, who was one of 1,200 immigrants who arrived in the UK from the controversial Red Cross-run Sangatte refugee camp in northern France in November 2002. Emad had travelled for three months to get to Sangatte, spent two months there and then was finally moved to a UK bed and breakfast where he shared a room with a friend he had made at Sangatte. Emad, who has a B.Sc., left Iraq not only because of persecution but also because he was paid a pittance – around US$3 per month. He came to the UK to start a new life. I last spoke to him as Christmas 2002 approached. 'It is frustrating to see things go so slowly, but I have kept hope that I will be able to live here. I keep being told that I will have to start at the bottom and cannot use my qualifications, which seems ridiculous.' He was also worried about how international relations between Britain and his country might affect him.

Other immigrants have been in the UK for years and are either unable or unwilling to work. Some have been lost in the vast bureaucratic system, others are just content to get what they can. However, to say there are lazy Turks, Afghans or Albanians is to miss the point. There are also lazy Scots, English, Welsh, French and Germans. No nation is perfect and no one is owed a living, so people who complain about immigrants should perhaps look first at their own kin.

But some of the strong emotions are easy to understand. In areas like Sighthill in Glasgow, Scotland, the council took in more than 1,000 immigrants, boosting the local population by more than a quarter and causing a lot of culture shock. To further add to the matter, many of the immigrants were given flats rent free – but that was not the biggest problem. It was when it was revealed that many of the immigrants had their flats equipped with what looked like brand-new furniture and utensils that jealousy really flared up.

One woman called Marie said: 'I've worked in the past. I'm unemployed just now but I always paid council taxes and so on, so why didn't I get a new couch or telly? I got given nothing from the council. Everything's second-hand.

'And you keep hearing that these people are all doctors and engineers and so on, so why don't we get them to work right away and other people – people who have paid taxes and are needy – can get these places? I've never seen a doctor need a council handout in my life.'

Tension mounted in Sighthill in August 2001, when Turkish Kurd Firsat Yildiz was killed one evening by a single stab wound. Some sections of the tabloid media portrayed him as a 'bogus' or 'economic' asylum seeker and tensions increased further.

A population's perception of immigrants is a matter their governments have to take into account, but at the same time they cannot pander to mob mentality. However, one thing that almost everyone agrees on was that the actual immigration system in the UK is terrible.

With this in mind, the Nationality, Immigration and Asylum Act 2002 was passed in November of that year. It brought in a number of new modern ideas, which included the closure of the Sangatte camp, doubling the number of work permits for low-skilled and seasonal labour, introducing citizenship ceremonies and a new citizenship pledge, requiring all new citizens to speak English or Welsh or Scottish Gaelic and have a knowledge and understanding of UK society.

It also gave British nationals who were living overseas during decolonisation a right to register as full British citizens and called for the establishment and operation of accommodation centres with basic services such as interpreters. The system is planned to work in such a way that, on arrival, asylum seekers will go to induction centres and remain there between one and seven days. Those who do not require further support (financial or information about how British society works) will then move to an agreed address, and others will move to accommodation centres.

Under the new law, those seeking support will stay in induction centres until their applications for support have been decided, at which time they will either be dispersed or sent to accommodation centres. In this new system, some asylum applications will be selected for fast-track processing. Asylum seekers will be detained in the centre while awaiting a decision, which should take no more than ten days. Those whose applications fail will be detained in removal centres until they can be deported.

The applicant will be interviewed about their history of persecution, and will have five days to present evidence to substantiate their claim. It is proposed that the Home Office should aim to make a decision on each application within two months and, if appealed, the courts aim to decide this within another four months, meaning everyone should be seen within seven months at the most.

The new law also requires asylum seekers living in the community to report regularly to offices or risk losing all government support. It also raised the prospect of toughening up the law to deal with smugglers and traffickers, with an increase in the penalty for facilitating illegal entry from ten to 14 years, putting it on a par with drug smuggling, and creating a new offence of trafficking for control over prostitution, also with a maximum of 14 years.

Of course, not everyone welcomes the new law. The Refugee Council claims it would not restore credibility to a heavily criticised asylum system, nor fundamentally improve decision-making or support asylum seekers in a sustainable or cost-effective way, and could even lead to more people being detained for longer than they need to be.

Perhaps the most famous migrant of them all to the UK is Mohamed Al Fayed, the owner of the famous store Harrods. Ever since he arrived in the UK in the early 1970s, Mr Al Fayed barely concealed his desire to be accepted into the establishment of his adopted country and regardless of opinions on the man – he is equally loved and loathed by many – it is not hard to see that the system is unfairly using him to suit itself.

His ambition to have a British passport and be a UK citizen is one that has seen him donate millions of pounds to British charities, assume control of Harrods and do many other deeds, including resurrecting the satirical magazine *Punch*. He has even moved into the mainstream British pursuit of football, buying Fulham FC and offering up the club's manager, Kevin Keegan, when the English national team was managerless.

Yet it seems the harder Mr Al Fayed has tried for acceptance, the more he has been brushed off. Mr Al Fayed has been refused citizenship and a passport a number of times, and no reason has ever been given despite the fact that he has four British children by his second wife, employs thousands of people and pays millions of pounds in tax to the UK Government. To add insult to injury, his brother Ali has been granted a UK passport by the Home Office. In March 2003, Mr Al Fayed decided to leave the UK for Switzerland following the termination of a long-standing agreement with the Inland Revenue. He commented, 'Why have I left? . . . Because I had no choice, effectively I've been forced out.'

Many other immigrants know how he feels.

PART 2

THE SMUGGLERS

7

A PROFESSIONAL SERVICE AT A PROFESSIONAL PRICE

'America is a fantastic country,' said Ko. 'It offers so much in the way of opportunities – even for those who do not go there.'

While many Chinese natives claim to know people who know someone who can help with moving to another country, speaking about it to an outsider is a completely different matter. A foreigner asking about people trafficking is likely to be an agent either of some government or police agency, neither of which are welcome. Anyone considering setting up their own smuggling concern will face many complications – some in the nature of physical injury – from already established lines in East Asia. Many people there are involved in people trafficking, from the Army and Government to the Triads and people in local villages. After the Army, it is probably one of the biggest employment areas in the region.

In Hong Kong, the situation is slightly more relaxed than elsewhere in Asia. Much of the vast amounts of money earned from people trafficking is spent there, where the East meets Western decadence. After many days of speaking to people – legal and not so legal – I was able to meet with Ko, who claimed not to be involved with Triads or with people smuggling, but knew people who were both. Contacts assured me that actually Ko was involved and his answers seem to back that up – as did the way he seemed to be very affluent, yet was never able to tell me what he did. He also provided details that were later corroborated by others. Despite his occasional assertion to 'have heard tales of . . .' I was left in no doubt by the end of our meetings that he was involved.

Ko claims not to be linked to the Triads who control most of the smuggling, 'though I am more than aware, and respectful, of them and make sure that our businesses do not clash. Ultimately, we end up dealing with a lot of the same people because so many people want to leave. But there are many groups involved in the smuggling businesses and the Western notion of Triads is very silly.' In the end, after much persuasion and many guarantees, Ko seems placated and is almost delighted to speak about his trade.

In the West, Triads are believed to be secret Chinese organisations dedicated to profits by criminal activities. Early 1990 estimates talked of 60 known Triads, with 12 major Triads. They were thought to be typified by and dis-tinguished from other criminal gangs by grouping into lodges with a hierarchical structure and traditional roles and titles. According to Ko, the West has it wrong.

'It is not all about a select few overseeing everyone else. It is a lot smaller. Triad societies are composed of small indi-vidual cells operating independently, all wanting to make money. Triad groups will fight each other if they must to control specific areas for their criminal activities, but they will also cooperate for financial gain. If everyone can make money, that is good. Triad membership serves primarily to facilitate introductions to other criminals and to help every-one work together.

'People smuggling is not an immoral business. People want to go somewhere and we help them. There is nothing more to it. We are not forcing anyone to do anything they do not want to. We are merely providing a service.'

Ko's theory has an almost Thatcherite or Reaganesque logic to it. All they are doing is exploiting a market. 'We will take someone anywhere they want to go . . . but it will cost them.'

Surely it should become cheaper if more and more people travel? Ko puts the constant rise in price down to the increasing methods needed to circumvent nations' security tactics.

'Yes, we charge what may be a lot of money but there are a lot of overheads and risks for us. After all, we go to jail if we are caught.'

Chinese efforts to stem the lucrative trade are often ineffective, according to Western agencies. However, China claims 98 people were imprisoned in 2000 for people-smuggling. In February 2001 authorities arrested about 400 human traffickers – there have been more since, but nothing on the scale of this. Ko's response is that every time one group stops helping people, others step in.

As Ko points out, they do not force people to go. People – who become known as *ren she* (human snake) – approach the *shetou* (snakehead groups) through people they know from *qinshu* (kinship) and *guanxi* (interactions and personal relationships). The cost of the trip is known as *bao* and it is this which has to be paid back.

According to Ko, four payment options are presented to most people who wish to be smuggled somewhere. The first is total payment up front. Second, 'a deposit is paid up front, with the balance to be paid on arrival by relatives or friends, who have co-signed as financial sponsors. The *ren she* will not leave the custody of our colleagues in the new land until the sum has been paid. This is proper and fair.

'If it is possible, the person can also arrange to work for our colleagues abroad, normally in a restaurant or factory for a set period of time – it can be up to 10 or 15 years I have heard – and they pay the cost back through manual labour.

'The last option is that of working for someone when in the new land and paying colleagues back with interest. For someone to do this, it has to be arranged through people who live in the new land.'

When I ask why, Ko is perfectly blunt about the reason: 'So the people owed money know who to go to when it is time to collect the debt or if the debtor should default.'

I ask Ko to tell me about this in more detail. Western media reports talk of brutalities and beatings, torture and worse. 'I cannot speak about what you say,' he claims. 'But you are thinking with a Western perspective. First of all, this is a business trip for all – those going and those providing the service. This is not gangsters like your "godfathers". Chinese are not surprised at being threatened when they don't pay up. In their minds, they have reneged on the deal and they would do anything not to be thought of as being unable to complete their end of the deal.'

But surely this is stacked against the person travelling, who may pay more than once to reach another land? 'No promises are ever made. It is only ever hoped that people will get to where they want to go.'

Another option for travelling, presented as a variation of the above methods, is for married Asian couples from elsewhere to get involved. According to Ko, there are a number of ways of doing this. The first sees the couple divorce and then get married to others in order to bring them into the new country as their husband or wife, though this is apparently becoming harder as time goes on.

Another method plays on Western stupidity, Ko relates with glee. 'A couple come over here and the husband goes back with a woman posing as his wife. The woman is not really his wife; she is merely posing and using the wife's passport. Then the passports are sent back here and a fake husband travels with the real wife. This works, thanks to the Western belief that many Asians all look the same. I have seen some couples earn more than US$60,000 by doing this, but again, as it involves flying, it is normally only the more affluent who get involved with this, but the fact that it works shows how poor your security still is. Not that I should complain.'

The last option is the most chilling, but it is an option that which allows a *ren she* to make money. They can carry something with them. In days gone by, this traditionally meant drugs but that has become very risky and few people choose that option. However, there is something else they can take with them that is far more valuable, and that is themselves – specifically, their livers, kidneys, lungs and other organs.

Ko does not look even mildly queasy over lunch as he describes this. 'There has been a rise in people willing to donate an organ in order to finance their trip. Most organs – and one time I heard a limb – will be considered. Anyone who does this will be given a genuine passport with a visa and sent over to America – that is the only country where we get requests for this – on the best of flights. They will also receive at least US$10,000, some of it up front if they want it for their family here.'

While all this treatment seems very pleasant, there is only one reason for it – to ensure that the organ that gets to the buyer is of the best quality. A person who has had to travel for weeks in filthy conditions may pick up an infection. A person travelling first-class is less likely to do so.

'When they arrive, they will be taken to a quiet place where the organ will be removed. Normally it is not done in a hospital. Giving an organ is also an option for those who have been in a new land and wish to pay off their debt and make a nice sum of money. There is more risk but there is also more reward.'

Whichever payment option is chosen, the next decision that has to be made is how to travel. Using genuine passports and visas and paying for an expensive flight is best, mainly because a person travelling first-class is less likely to be stopped at customs, or to be suspected by immigration officials, as they will be well-dressed and groomed. Next in price is the choice of flying economy, still with a passport and visa. Below that, come travelling by boat or a long land journey by car. 'It all comes down to one thing – cost,' states Ko nonchalantly.

Bizarrely, in many cases of people leaving a contract called a *renqing* is signed before any departure. This covers such matters as a deposit, who the guarantors are and so on. Ko and his associates have their own preferences for the sorts of travel they arrange. 'It is easier to arrange to go to America. Much more easy than the West of Europe unless flying – but most who can afford that, want America.'

Ko is obviously reluctant to reveal the tricks that they (or rather the people he has heard of being involved) use, but they are myriad and some of them would not look out of place in a James Bond film. The depths or, rather, the 'heights' of complicity were beyond my expectation. 'It is not easy to get a boatful or a busload of people out of the country. Of course there are others involved. Everyone is respectful of everyone else's business and some will help out if the price is good. Of course, some are not and may try to sabotage your efforts.'

This does not apply only to other snakehead gangs. At our last meeting Ko revealed one of the most surprising facts about who helps the smugglers. 'We learn a lot from our friends in the People's Liberation Army who help many for a good price, especially in the Guangdong province where there are many ports. They cannot be stopped. Customs police would not dare to stop an Army vehicle.'

According to other Chinese sources, this fact is known only in certain military circles outside China – news of any smuggling cases involving the armed forces is forbidden to be published, which means the story is rarely heard further afield either. What is known is that in 1998 a military court in Guangzhou sentenced a squad commander to death and a political officer to jail for 10 years for protecting smugglers. Army prosecutors claimed the two men had ordered soldiers to fire on customs police during confrontations in the South China Sea.

'The Army are the biggest criminals here. People go on about the triads. They are nothing compared to the Army and Navy. Vehicles are stolen from Hong Kong. I have a right-hand drive car myself. Even impounded vehicles are available for the right price. Cigarettes, computers and software are also all easily brought in. But *people* have to bring them. They do not walk in by themselves. They are also excellent trading items.

'The Chinese Navy does not make a habit of stopping boats for no reason – unlike the British who were a nuisance up until the day they left in 1997. The Army and Navy do not get directly involved in moving people, but it is not unheard of for people to be taken from a military boat to another ship out at sea, or for military vehicles to take people from towns across the land to the docks. No one stops a military vehicle.

'You also have to remember that various people in the Army own or part-own more than 1,500 hotels and not everyone can get to a dock within a day's travel. I have heard that very often the Army and Navy are excellent partners to do business with, not just in the case of moving people to the sea. It can also be handy to let them know when your ship is moving so that it is not disturbed, or perhaps even to tell them when a competitor's ship is moving . . .'

Even more worrying, it's not just the Army and Navy. Ko claims the Chinese Government agency, the Public Security Bureau (PSB), are also involved.

'Think about it,' he says, as if it is the most natural thing. 'This is a boon for everyone here, not only because it helps get rid of unemployment – a person who had a job leaves, someone here gets the job, which is good – it also allows for a cut down on population and, even better, money is sent back to the local economies as people provide for their families. This is not crime, this is working with the powers in command.'

When I tell Ko that I am not convinced, that he must take me for a poor sucker *gaijin* (foreigner), he points out one thing: 'Many people travel with passports. Where would we get them all? How could so many other things happen: the knowledge of shipping lanes, the times when it is easy to get past checkpoints? Everything is connected to the top levels and the more people who go to America, the more they may be able to have influence there.

'Money already allows for influence elsewhere – countries like Belize, Mexico and Taiwan have all been helpful at times. Ministers and people who work in immigration are always prime targets and once they accept one payment from you, you have them forever because you have nothing to lose, but they can go to jail.'

Other reports do seem to support Ko's claims, at least to some extent. Former Deputy Secretary-General of China's Xinhua news agency, Wong Man-Fong, admitted that in the early 1980s he had 'befriended' Hong Kong's Triad bosses at Beijing's behest: 'Beijing explained to the Triad bosses that they would be left alone by Chinese authorities if they ceased their activities during the handover,' former Hong Kong legislator James To told the *New American* magazine. 'So the Triad leaders called a temporary truce in order to "give face" to Beijing while the world was watching.'

Mr To, who was the chair of the legislature's internal security committee, added: 'China's Public Security Bureau and the other mainland law enforcement agencies are more like business partners than enemies of the Triads. There are security and intelligence personnel involved in all of the Triad's illegal activities, including drug smuggling, alien-smuggling and vice. Some of this simply reflects the personal corruption of some isolated officials, but a lot of it takes place with the connivance of high-ranking people in the Party.'

Another person involved in the trade who preferred anonymity added this: 'The Americans are incredibly stupid in fighting this because they think that all of the Chinese authorities want the same goals as them. That is not the case. Some people will be fighting it, but others in the same organisations are getting access to all the plans for combating the smuggling, allowing them to work round it. The Americans provide the information to defeat themselves.'

However, the USA has made one major arrest when Cheng Chui-Ping or 'Big Sister Ping', also known as the 'Mother of All Snakeheads', was arrested in 2000 and extradited to the USA for trial in 2002. Ping is the alleged ringleader of a global people-smuggling racket, based in New York's Chinatown district. Her arrest was the result of a tip off from Interpol, where an alert researcher had spotted the name of Ping's son on the reservations list for a flight to New York. Like a good Chinese mother, Ping had insisted on seeing him off and was caught by 40 agents as she did so.

The US Immigration and Naturalization Service (INS) and the FBI allege that Ping allied herself with Chinese gangsters to develop an international trade in more than 3,000 people over a period of 20 years, building a fortune of US$30 million in the process, and being responsible for more than a dozen deaths that occurred on voyages to the USA that she allegedly organised. Agents pursuing Ping suspected that she even had links to the snakehead ring involved in the horrific deaths of 58 Chinese in a sealed container lorry at Dover in 2000 recounted in chapter 1, but this has not been proved.

What has surprised the USA is that many Chinese people feel loyalty and respect – not stemming from fear – for Ping. An INS source said: 'Without exaggeration, she was worshipped for what she did to bring people to the USA. OK, she was breaking the law, but love and respect for the family always comes first in China, and you would happily hand your last dollar to Sister Ping to be reunited.'

Ping's story is one that many Chinese know. Indeed, she is an inspiration to many. She had somehow acquired American citizenship – investigators speculate that forgery was involved – which gave her the right to be joined by her husband and son. According to documents filed with the US District Court in Manhattan, by the mid-1980s Ping had already put together her smuggling network, travelling periodically to China to build up contacts with corrupt officials and establishing links with underworld suppliers of forged passports and travel papers. She ensured that everyone from senior government officials and policemen to taxi drivers and petty bureaucrats owed her a favour. She also built links in the USA, including with the notorious Fuk Ching gang.

By charging US$18,000 for each journey, she was making half of that in profit, not including interest from people who were not able to pay immediately. In 1985 her husband, Cheng Yick-Tak, was bringing in a group of four passengers on a dinghy. But the four drowned when it swept too close to Niagara Falls. He was charged with criminal conspiracy; he took the rap alone and served nine months in jail. But this did not deter Ping.

Her alleged business took a massive boost in 1991 when President George Bush granted amnesty for all Chinese then living illegally in the USA in the aftermath of the Tiananmen Square massacre in Beijing. This produced a fresh surge of people wanting to bring relatives and friends out of China to the USA. But she did not keep all of the money, funding community centres for the needy.

FBI interest in her continued to build and US chiefs believe her downfall started in 1993 when Ping and several other snakeheads combined to bring in an unusually large shipment of 300 Fujianese on a run-down freighter. The head of the Fuk Ching gang, a much-feared thug known as Ah Kay, had won the vessel in a poker game. Renamed *Golden Venture* for the voyage, it arrived safely off the New England coast but arrangements to unload it were disrupted at the last moment by the death of two of Ah Kay's brothers in a gangland shootout.

According to court papers, the ship's master was ordered to beach it wherever he could. On 6 June the vessel ran aground in rough seas off the Rockaway Peninsula in the

New York borough of Queens. Police launches rescued most of those aboard, but a number of terrified immigrants drowned or died of hypothermia within sight of the shore that they had risked so much to reach.

Although efforts were increased from then on, it took until 2000 for Ping to be caught and until 2002 for Hong Kong to agree to extradite her to the USA, where she faces a life sentence if found guilty of all the alleged crimes.

Even though Ping is in custody, people smuggling continues and there are many ways of doing it. Ko seems to know many of them.

'One of the best things I ever heard of was when a group were smuggled in, posing as a group of experts for an art exhibition. The smugglers went as far as to actually book a hall and so on for the event for added authenticity. Very often though, when dealing with a group, you have them pose as tourists or a group of businessmen, saying they are over to look at investment. In some areas, just saying that will get you through as the authorities are desperate for money and jobs to come to the area.'

Sea travel, he claims, is the best. 'Escape by sea is much easier and cheaper. There are many ways to do it, including having the travellers ferried from the coastline to international waters, and then transferred at sea to the smuggling vessel. Alternatively, they can be ferried to a sparsely populated island to await the arrival of the smuggling ship. Some even go direct on Taiwanese or Hong Kong ocean-going ships, fishing vessels, coastal junks or cargo boats that have legitimate access to Fujian or Guangzhou ports. Taiwanese ships are being used less at the moment as the authorities were stopping them most frequently.'

What the people do on the boat depends on what they have paid. Some will be allowed to roam the boat, only hiding when need be; some will not. One thing that is less common now is having people pose as members of crew because everyone needs papers now, even crew, and these are checked off on pre-sent manifest lists.

However, there is still one situation that sees the crew being comprised of immigrants: when the ship is abandoned. Ko explains this in great detail, grinning at many points during his account, as if to imply that parts of the story are not what they seem.

'A fishing company will "hire" a group of people for a trip. The boat will then set sail across the Pacific and the cargo bay will be filled with fish. Then the crew will mutiny. Unknown to the captains, many of the crew have brought little boats with them, or taken small boats from the ship, and they will abandon the big ship when it is near somewhere like America or Canada, Guam, Australia or New Zealand.

'The captain of course recovers from the shock – or perhaps even has to work himself loose from being tied up – and contacts the authorities eventually. There will be some questions but at some point he has to take his fish-laden boat back home. It is so sad for the captains. They cannot find decent crews these days. But they do not end up poor and at the end of the day they cannot be arrested for anything if they stay in international waters.'

One trick that Ko is happy to reveal – 'because it is no longer used' – involves hollowed-out boats. This would see boatloads of illegal travellers go from a larger boat in international waters to a country's shores. If the boats were captured, they'd be towed to shore and those passengers on view taken away. The boats – which looked like rotting boxes or pieces of wood just thrown together – would often be abandoned. Later, when everyone was gone, other immigrants (who had paid more) would get out of a false bottom of the boat and make their escape to the new land. 'That was a great method,' laments Ko, 'but coast guards now tow boats right to land or examine them thoroughly. It rarely works now.'

But the smugglers are not standing still. Among their latest plans are some of their most audacious yet. One American politician with a strong interest in Sino–American affairs believes there will be more and more waterfronts bought up in order to aid smuggling – and not just of people.

'Not all of the money earned in America can be laundered back so some are now investing it in land, but not just any land. They are buying up ports and docks, especially as many of these go out of business. Now, if you own the docks, it is a lot easier to bring people in and ship them out to safe houses than it is to bring them in to a dock that is not owned by a group. This is where we see the next development being – it is the next logical step – but there is nothing we can do as it is all presented as a perfectly legal business venture, especially if it includes investment from a Far East shipping operation. It's been dubbed the "Coca-Cola plan". Just as Coke own everything from the factories to the trucks used to distribute the goods, so smugglers can do the same.'

Sinologist Nicholas Eftimiades has also warned of a more dangerous possibility. In his report *Chinese Intelligence Operations*, he claims that accepting Chinese business at face value is dangerously naïve. He asserts that most companies in the People's Republic of China are subservient adjuncts of the Communist Party and the Ministry of State Security (MSS), the Chinese equivalent of the KGB, which – when you consider the "Coca-Cola plan" – ties everything together insidiously.

But Ko and others like him have no intention of going anywhere – unlike the thousands of people they take money from each year – and Ko is not embarrassed to admit it. 'Why should I?' he asks, sipping expensive Scotch. 'I have an excellent lifestyle here. If others want to go that is their concern. Why would I want to leave? I can use my talents here. There is no need for me to make life hard for myself.'

8

WILY COYOTES

South America is a fantastic continent to visit as a tourist. From Rio de Janeiro to Mexico City, there are stunning examples of both natural beauty and human talents. Unfortunately, not all of these talents are put to good or, rather, legal use.

South America is an amazing place to live if you have money. Sadly, money is something that not many every-day people have there. It has always been the poor relation of its northern cousin and, as such, people want to move on to places where the weather may not be as good, but they believe there's more chance of actually making money.

Just as there is no shortage of people trying to get in to the USA, there is no shortage of people wanting to help them get in. There are a number of ways in through the south but the most popular by far is via Mexico. Unlike those in many other parts of the world the smugglers in Mexico are a lot more open about their service, but the big players rarely make themselves known. It is their 'field agents', for lack of a better term, who are out talking, trying to see if people want to be moved.

Alcocer – 'Call me Al' – was one such person, telling me that I would get across easily if I wanted to be smuggled. 'We could put you in a passenger seat – or even have you drive a car and pretend that you were a lost tourist. White people are easy to move.'

People like Al do not see themselves as bad people. 'I am providing a service. People come to me and ask for help to move and that's what I do. The Americans should also be grateful. They spend a lot on border guards. I keep them all in a job as they try to find the people we take over. We keep their economy going by giving them all jobs, and the people who come back here keep our economy going. Everyone wins.'

Al may think he is a coyote – the local term for someone who guides or takes people from Mexico into America – but he doesn't take anyone across the border. He's been caught too many times doing it, so he has others to do that part for him. Nor is he the boss. Mexican smuggling has become too lucrative for small operators. Like people smuggling elsewhere, it's the big operators who run the show now, seeing the preferred and easier profit to be made from people than drugs. Many of the small-time operators were given the chance to join up, leave town or take rather more unpleasant options. According to Al, 'I used to run here, then I was given some choices. This choice gives me a good life.'

What Al does is perhaps the most important part of the operation: he helps everyone get in touch. He finds people who want to move to America – or they find him. He takes the money, minus his commission, and passes it on to someone else who will pass it on again. To call him a *tick-eteros* would be more accurate, though he believes he is a coyote. He will also tell the people who paid him where they should be and what they should have with them. It's a high-profile job, making him the man most likely to be arrested if the authorities clamp down. But as long as he stays in Mexico he's fairly safe. The authorities there are unlikely to bother him, thanks to his job's connections. The human-smuggling business is yet to experience fights on the same scale as the drug turf wars.

But from the first meeting, Al is also doing something else: working out how to get people across the border. There are 'many ways to do it. Many tricks and many ways of paying. It is up to a person how much they want to pay. If they want we can fly them in. We can get them passports, computers help us make documents. We have mobile phones that will dial numbers in America where people will answer and say they know the person at the other end. We can give them good clothes . . . many ways and things to do to convince.'

At the other end of the scale, where money is tight, Al says there are a number of options. For example, people can chance climbing a wall and running, hoping to get somewhere using a poor map and nothing more. That costs US$1,000, which 'covers the cost of the knowledge, the map and a bottle of water.' Another option is getting caught. As ridiculous as this sounds, it's used quite a lot.

'The ones who cannot afford to go, we send them out straight into the arms of the guards or near the guards. That way the guards are diverted and distracted while we get the others in. Once they have done that a few times then we take them across, but nothing fancy. If they want something fancy they have to take some packages over for other people, but being caught with them is very risky.'

The 'package' is normally drugs but there have been times when it has been something else, including babies being taken across to their parents.

In between deliberately being caught and flying in style, people have the option of being smuggled in by car ('An average car can earn you a lot of money as you can get three people into a car trunk and a fourth behind a dashboard. You can also get one into a seat but this is a little more tricky. But one trip can earn you over US$10,000 profit,' enthuses Al), or on lorries and trailer trucks. Prices for this start at over US$3,000 and rise depending on how you want to be smuggled in. NAFTA laws forbid trailer trucks being physically searched so if a lorry manages to avoid an X-ray scan, the people inside it are away free. Diesel trucks are also very popular. A part of the tanker will be compartmentalised and lined with benches for people to sit on. The only danger there is air-supply problems but some smugglers claim to have found ways round this.

In some places there are tunnels, which can be used to go from one country to the next. The local environment can also play a part in determining how people try to sneak over. For example, in Calexico, Mexico, people will try to float down a stream that is loaded with toxic chemicals and sewage. The illegal immigrants hope that the border patrol won't jump in to try to pull them out – but they also hope that they themselves won't fall in.

Al may be the middle rung on the ladder of smuggling and there is competition, but for him it is friendly competition because there are so many still trying to get in. America is a growth industry for Al and his compatriots. He has just learned a new trick, which he will have to use at some point. It is rather cheap, in more ways that one.

'I heard of people who take pictures of prostitutes – or someone else – naked, and they give these pictures to some of the drivers in cars. So you have a car with a man and a woman up front – and others hiding in the trunk or elsewhere. You drive up when it is busy and, if you are stopped, the man hands over his documents but at the same time the picture falls to the ground – accidentally, of course.' He coughs conspiratorially. 'The man pulls a face and starts to act panicked to get the picture back. Naturally the guard will look at what it is. As that happens, the woman in the car starts to get angry and either cries a lot or starts shouting and hitting the man.

'Now if it's busy enough the guard is just going to wave them through because the last thing he needs is for people to be fighting and arguing so much and holding everything else up. He will also have been distracted by seeing a naked lady and that could affect him in a number of ways. It is a good scheme, I like it. We may give the travelling woman a discount if she does the pose, otherwise we use someone else.'

But what if, I ask, it's a woman at the border check? 'They are lesbians so it would do the same to them,' is his unsavoury answer. 'No pretty or normal woman would do their job.'

Al's attitude is like that of many others. Whereas many of the Chinese and East Asian smugglers most of the time appeared to be acting on a professional business level, Mexican smuggling feels a lot more seedy. One reason for that may be the large numbers of women who are moved about as sex slaves. According to the CIA and State Department, an estimated 50,000 women are trafficked into the United States annually, most as sex slaves and many of them from Mexico.

Al doesn't deny that he plays a part in it. 'Yes, I move women. Some of them are fed up here and want to move on elsewhere. Some think they can be actresses. Some want to escape partners who beat them, but you have to be careful about moving them because the partner could come after you and you don't know who he knows.'

Al will not talk about women he knows of who have been forced to become sex slaves, claiming he has heard such tales but has never had any proof. I found his attempt at excuses unconvincing. While you could think that Al and others like him are gentlemanly rogues, engaged in games of chess with the authorities, there are others who will remind you exactly what this business is about. And many of them suffered at the hands of one family – the Cadenas.

Isa had been a pretty 21-year-old working as a lemon picker and a cleaner when she decided to try for life in America to earn more money for her family. When she returned two years later, she was pregnant, two members of her family were dead and the rest had been forced to move to another town hundreds of miles away. All because she had wanted to help.

Many of the Cadenas are synonymous with people smuggling. Their operation started back in the 1980s, where they promised to take people over the border for a few thousand dollars a time. According to the US State Department, it was girls they transported, from Vera Cruz, Mexico, through Matamoros, Mexico to Brownsville, Texas and Florida. They smuggled Isa to South Florida, 'mostly through bribes and hiding in one truck for a few hours', she recalls.

It had not been easy to get that far, though. A coyote working for the Cadenas had visited her town and said that they would be taking people away if they wanted to go. Normally people had to travel to the larger towns and cities to get help from smugglers but one of the tactics the Cadenas used was to visit small towns and offer to take people away. Not everyone worked for the Cadenas, but many did and others just used their name. The effect was the same: people left their homes, villages and towns.

Isa convinced her family to let her go so that she could send money back and allow the family to buy land. She had heard of jobs as nannies, baby-sitters and other tasks that would allow her to send back a good sum every week. She hoped she would be able to earn up to US$200 a week. One of her uncles had wanted to travel with her, but she said she would be fine and also pointed out that they could not afford another person going – she already had to pay the smugglers back completely when she reached America, before sending money back home.

Once in Florida, Isa was told she could stay at a safe house before she was found a job and a place to stay, but the house was anything but safe. Police later revealed that a number of homes in areas like Fort Pierce, Okeechobee, Avon Park, Palm Beach, Lake Worth and Fort Myers were used and it is likely that Isa was in one of them.

'We were forced into having sex with a lot of men,' Isa recalled. 'There were two other girls with me and we were all saying we weren't there for sex. The men hit us with pistols and gang-raped us and told us that was what we would be doing from now on. I still cannot get the horror of that day out of my head. The men stank of sweat and were rough, bristly, fat-bellied. It was all over in about 20 minutes and afterwards we all just cried constantly.

'From the next day, we were all put in little rooms that seemed little bigger than coffins – all they had in them was a single bed and a bucket with water and a cloth, so we could be clean – and men would come in every 20 minutes or so and take us.

'What made it worse was that many of the men were South American. One of the girls said that a man from her hometown took her and all he said was that he had had his eye on her years ago. He knew her and did nothing. None of them did.'

Thirty men a day each was not unusual at US$20 a time, of which the women were given US$3. Of course the guards did not pay for the sex they took when no one else was about. They weren't the only ones who didn't pay, according to Isa. 'A couple of different police officers were known to come in as well and take us. One of them was known for hitting us and calling us a lot of names.'

What Isa didn't know then was that having people come in dressed as police is another regular tactic used to keep women in her situation docile. The women get the feeling that the police are as untrustworthy as anyone else and it stops them running off to the authorities. While the police who eventually liberated Isa claim that the police officers were false, Isa still isn't sure. She trusts no one.

Another tactic used involved sheets of paper Isa had signed during her journey. She was told that they were for contact details and banking forms so money could be sent back home but, as her English was poor, she did not question what she was signing.

She was told that a paper she had signed on the journey was a confession that she had stolen US$5,000. If she managed to leave, she was warned, this piece of paper would end up back home and she would be disgraced. It would also be said that she had tried to seduce people and break up marriages.

Isa was a slave for over a year, earning roughly US$200,000 for her bosses. She never saw her share. She was told how much she had and, if she wanted something, someone would go to buy it and deduct the cost from her savings. She was helping the Cadenas earn a fortune. It has been estimated that 40 women earned the family and their associates US$2.5 million during a two-year period.

Isa earned them money in other ways apart from sex. From the papers she had signed on the journey, others were allowed to get fraudulent credit cards and run them up.

One of the more soul-destroying parts of her existence was the younger girls, some of whom were 11 and 12. They begged for help but there was nothing Isa could do. One girl in particular chilled her. 'This girl did not complain about what happened to her. She just thought this was normal and had accepted it as what happened to everyone. I found that horrific.'

Meanwhile back home, rumours did start to circulate as people wondered why their children had not been in touch. The worry took its toll on Isa's father, who died as a result of the stress. 'Of course I did not know this. I also didn't find out that when my uncle went to confront people about everything, he was beaten up and his home burnt down, with his elderly mother-in-law inside. It was after that my family moved. Shame had a lot to do with that. There was shame on their behalf about what might have happened to me but there was also shame that they couldn't do anything. I know my uncle thought about killing himself.'

But in Florida, the girls were doing what they could to survive. They tried to keep condom wrappers as their own way of working out how much of their debt they might have paid off, but the bundles were always discovered and destroyed.

'One girl started marking herself with small nicks to try to work it out as well but she ended up infecting her foot – she had to make the marks where they couldn't be seen – and spent days in bed. That did not stop men being sent into her, though. She also fell pregnant and an abortion was performed on the bed. The cost was added to what she already owed. After the abortion she was given a day's rest, then the sheets were changed and men came back. One of the guards said that they should have let her stay pregnant for longer, as some men paid more for that.'

Isa's freedom came when others managed to escape a Cadena whorehouse and get help from the FBI after they reached the Mexican consulate. Between November 1997 and February 1998, raids closed three Cadena brothels and found others that had been used in the past. A number of women from Veracruz and *ticketeros* were arrested. Further raids and police work brought in others across Florida, including dens in Boynton Beach and West Palm Beach.

It took weeks – and in some cases months – for the women to trust the agents, but eventually details of what had happened under the Cadenas were passed on. During this time, which the women spent in jail, threats managed to reach them. It was also here that Isa learned what had happened to her family. After they had given all their evidence, they were told that the Florida Immigrant Advocacy Center in Miami would help them process any applications to stay in America, but Isa wanted to go back to her family. She eventually found them, but life has not been easy since as she is still scarred from what she went through and has received no support from the Mexican authorities.

As a result of police finding Isa and the others, some of the Cadenas were put behind bars. Rogerio Cadena, one of the uncles and main leaders in the family, was arrested in early 1998 on charges of slavery. He pleaded guilty to violating the civil rights of women under the 12th Amendment, which bans slavery and involuntary servitude, though he maintained all throughout the trial in 1999 that he was not a major player in the operation.

As well as doing time, Rogerio and the others were ordered to pay US$1million in compensation to their victims. The way the formula was worked out was that the number of weeks the women had been sex slaves was multiplied by the price they charged for sex multiplied by 132, which was perceived to be the amount of times each women had sex in a week – a number most now believe to have been lower than the actuality. But Rogerio claimed to have no money and has yet to pay any compensation to the women.

Six members of the Cadena family charged in the indictment remain at large. The fugitives are Juan Luis Cadena, Carmen Cadena, Rafael Alberto Cadena, Abel Cadena, Antonio Sosa and Patricio Sosa. They are believed to be in Mexico. A US State Department insider told me, 'I'll be damn surprised if some, if not all, of them aren't up to their old tricks. They'll have just learned some new things to try and stay ahead of us, but they aren't the only problem or the only people doing this.'

One woman, called Maria, was a Mexican sex slave. She now lives in America, but she is so scared of the Cadenas that she refuses to return to Mexico. She lives in fear after telling the authorities what she has gone through and identifying the people who did it.

It was in 1997 in Veracruz, Mexico, that 18-year-old Maria was approached by an acquaintance about some jobs in the United States. She was told there were jobs available in restaurants and that she would earn enough money to support her daughter and her parents in Mexico. She accepted the offer and a coyote took her to Texas. There it all changed.

'I was transported to Florida and there one of the bosses told me I would be working in a brothel as a prostitute. I told him he was mistaken and that I was going to be working in a restaurant, not a brothel. He said I owed him a smuggling debt and the sooner I paid it off the sooner I could leave.

'I was constantly guarded and abused. If any of the girls refused to be with a customer, we were beaten. If we adamantly refused, the bosses would show us a lesson by raping us brutally. We worked six days a week, 12 hours a day. Our bodies were sore and swollen. If anyone became pregnant she was forced to have an abortion. The cost of the abortion was added to the smuggling debt.'

Escape was never an option because the people running things kept them unsettled and on the move. 'The bosses carried weapons. They scared me. I never knew where I was. We were transported every 15 days to different cities. I knew if I tried to escape I would not get far because everything was unfamiliar. The bosses said that if we escaped they would get their money from our families.

'I was enslaved for several months; other women were enslaved for up to a year. But it all finally ended when the INS, FBI and local law enforcement raided the brothels and rescued us. After I was released from my captors, I cooperated with the government to send some of the slave drivers to jail. Some of them are serving sentences in the United States but unfortunately others are free in Mexico, threatening our families. Meanwhile I continue to wait for my "S" visa [a visa for those providing information regarding crimes and terrorism] and the one for my daughter. She will be six years old. I have not seen her since I left my country when she was only a year and half.

'I never thought this process would take so long. Seven of our captors were successfully prosecuted in 1999. 2002 is coming to its end and we are all waiting for a status that would allow us to remain safe in the United States and also to give us the opportunity to be reunited with our loved ones. My desire to see my daughter and the chance to give her a better life keep me going. But how long do we have to wait?

'If I had had the opportunity to apply for a "T" visa [for victims of trafficking for illicit sexual purposes and slavery] I understand that the transition to the life I lead now in this country would have been significantly less burdensome. Once INS gave me work authorisation, I went out looking for employment, without knowing the city, without speaking the language, without any guidance. My goal was to obtain honest employment immediately to send money to my parents for my daughter's upbringing. From that day I have not stopped. I continue to work for the same company that hired me when I was most desperate.

'But my story is not the story of most of the women and girls that were enslaved by the Cadena family. Most of the women are struggling to rebuild their lives. Some are mothers, who do not count on any form of assistance with day care because of their present immigration status and that of their children. They do not have any special training that would help them obtain employment, which would provide for day care.'

Vicente is, unlike Al, still a genuine coyote. He goes across the border. He too is no longer his own boss but he welcomes the new way of doing things. 'In the mid-1990s it was everyone going their own way and teaming up to help each other if you had to, more often you just went alone with the people you were leading.

'Now thanks to the guards working harder, everyone else has to work harder. Things are run more like a business. If someone else does something for me, I'll be charged for their time and any expenses. I do the same back.'

Vicente does not fear arrest and a look at the figures shows why. In 2000, 1,858 arrests were made on coyotes. The following year it was down by 500 and on average over the last eight years has been generally diminishing, leaving Vicente to make the point: 'They are not putting us off the job by catching us and we are not retiring thanks to the money we make, so the only other conclusion is that they are getting worse at their job. To be fair, we are getting better at avoiding them as well thanks to modern technology, and I don't mean the people on the radio. I know of coyotes out there who use laptops to send emails and details every few hours if they know something. They also use it to advise of conditions. Email's great for that. It's a lot harder for them to intercept an email than a radio call or voice call on a phone.'

Vicente works out of Villa Zapata, a place full of coyotes. In fact it could well be Mexico's capital of smuggling. One reason for this is that the expert border police and patrol were taken away in 2001. No one knows why, but many have their suspicions, claiming a police bribe. 'Nonsense,' says Vicente. 'The operators here do not bribe the police – that would be setting your sights too low. Money does change hands but not to anyone that low down. You don't give the cops the money, you give it to the people who give them instructions, though some grunt cops will see something if they help us. If you were ever lifted you were rarely off the streets for more than a day and you never gave a proper address. But now there is no one with jurisdiction over what we do, as the normal police certainly don't bother us. Hell, some of them have asked us for advice on moving.'

The local newspaper *La Crónica* revealed how bad the problem was in 2001 when it reported that different police stations and other organisations were fighting over who would receive protection money from the coyotes.

'It's a great time to be doing this job. Everything's on our side and I think it's only going to get better. People always want to get into America. They see the dream of making it big. Me? I don't need to go there, I'm making it well here.'

But not everyone wants to go to the USA, especially post-11 September 2001. The smugglers have seen more demand for Europe, which of course is also more expensive. One trick that South Americans (and Africans too) have found quite useful to get into Europe is to claim to be a footballer. This scandal came to light in the UK in 2000 after Arsenal announced in the summer that they had signed talented midfielder Edu from Corinthians for £6 million. It seemed a great boost for the club but problems developed at Heathrow Airport when immigration officers refused to let him in.

There was immediate confusion over the issue. The Home Office put out a statement saying: 'We can confirm a Brazilian national was refused entry to the UK when he was found to be in possession of a counterfeit passport.' An insider told the *Daily Mirror* that the passport was 'Around the same standard as something you might have learned to make on [the children's TV show] *Blue Peter*.'

Arsenal made no statement about a false passport. They said: 'Unbeknown to both parties, there was a problem with Edu's passport and, consequently, he has returned to Brazil where the situation can be resolved.' Edu's agent chimed in, saying: 'There were no false documents. Some were missing, so Edu returned to Brazil to get the documents requested. Edu has Portuguese and Italian ancestors, and as such has a right to play in the European Union.'

It must have taken a lot of searching for the documents because the matter rumbled on for six months before the player signed for Arsenal saying: 'I am so happy because I have managed to prove that I am as good as my word. I am an honest person and appreciate that Arsenal gave me time to prove that. I can hold my head up high. I knew I qualified for a Portuguese passport because my grandmother was born there.'

But just as everyone was about to forget that there had ever been claims of a false passport, he said: 'I don't know who falsified my passport.'

It wasn't the first time it had happened in English football. Argentinian player Esteban Fuertes was originally allowed into the UK to play for Derby but was refused entry after returning from a club trip to Portugal, where it was discovered that he was travelling on a forged Italian passport. He never returned to the club, but did end up with a French work permit.

Football bosses FIFA and UEFA have mounted a number of investigations into the phenomenon. In England, Gordon Taylor, chief executive of the Professional Footballers' Association, has warned of the issue, saying in 2002: 'If they cannot get in by fair means, they will try to get in by foul. People believe English football is dripping with money and it is making the game here a honey-pot for agents and players all around the world. The public cases of what seems like passport forgery to get a player into the country could just have been the tip of the iceberg. And it is not the only way they try to get in. We have our suspicions that marriages have been arranged to give people the right to get in.

'This is what will happen in an era when clubs are buying ready-made teams from abroad. There is a network of agents out there ready to cash in on that by any means possible.'

Top English football agent Jon Smith, who used to represent the England team, explained what he called a 'black market'. He said: 'They have a different way of doing business in South America. The culture is very different. A lot of it is just the way things are done. A lot of it is corruption. But what people here would see as a scam would not be seen in the same light there – it would be seen as gaining an advantage. It is also the case that a lot of players are "owned" by many different agents. The clubs are poor so they sell off slices of their young talent to keep going – with the buyer getting a slice of any future transfer fee.

'You also have a situation where a lot of politicians are involved in football, so it can be easy to get hold of fake documents. The same is true of players coming from Africa.'

The Brazilians were quick to point out that the Edu incident was not all their own fault and tried to pass some of the blame over to European clubs. During Congressional hearings into corruption in Brazilian football in 2001, one of the main investigators, Aldo Rebelo, said: 'Without denying Brazilian clubs' responsibility – we have facts which show the part managers, agents and European clubs played in the false passport scandal.'

In 2001, French club St Etienne were docked seven points and one of their vice-presidents was banned for a year over a fake passport scandal involving Brazilian striker Alex and goalkeeper Maxim Levitsky, a man of confused nationality. Alex alleged he was shown a Portuguese passport by the club and forced to sign it to stay in the side, saying: 'They guaranteed it was a legal passport, took care of photographs and administration duties. My agents suspected straightaway that it was a fake and told me not to use it.'

Levitsky, a goalkeeper qualified for both Ukraine and Russia, actually played on a counterfeit Greek passport. He said in a court hearing that it was his own decision to use the fake document.

The Spanish Football Federation, RFEF, also mounted investigations into a number of players including Delio Cesar Toledo, Barata and Federico Basavilbaso of Tenerife, Gustavo Bartlet of Rayo Vallecano, Amarilla of Getafe, and Moya of Granada as part of a wide-reaching look at the problem of false passports.

Italian giants Inter Milan found themselves in trouble after being found guilty of knowingly fielding Uruguayan Alvaro Recoba on a false Italian passport, while Udine police accused Paraguayan Alejandro Da Silva and Brazilians Warley and Alberto of having false passports.

But while the moving around of adults on false passports is bad enough, the Brazilian investigations found something even more sinister – the trafficking of young Brazilian foot-ballers who were still school-age children. The hearings uncovered the case of Fabio Farias, a talented 16-year-old footballer whose family were paid US$3,000 by an agent to arrange a move to Belgium for him. This money was also to pay for a fake passport 'to make things easier for him', which meant making it easier for him to be signed by a top club and therefore earn the big money that is lacking in most of South American football. Fabio probably had little choice in deciding whether to sign with this agent – the money paid by the agent to Fabio's family being nothing compared to the fortune he'd make from deals involving the player.

Fabio told the hearings that, along with other children, he stayed in Belgium for eight months in one flat with no money. They were given only food they had to cook them-selves. Then, one day, their 'agent' vanished and they were discovered by the authorities, who sent them home.

The hearings were told that there were more than 10,000 Brazilians playing professional football in other countries across the world. It was not known how many had fake passports and credentials to 'make things easier' so that they could one day make the big money. The hearings also heard allegations that diplomatic officials at the highest level were involved while Brazilian club presidents helped earn their vast personal fortunes by illegal selling of players. It is not only a South American problem – it also happens in Africa, where players are smuggled out of countries such as Ghana, sometimes in the boot of a car, to join teams in Europe.

South America does suffer from many of the same problems as Africa – not least poverty – and people will continue to want to leave. As long as they do, people like Al and Vicente, backed by people and groups like the Cadenas, will help them.

9

THE EUROPEAN FAMILY BUSINESS

European smugglers are a different type of human trafficker again. Chinese smugglers often have a personal connection in the line of people who help others to move and, once the money has been exchanged, the process is conducted like a normal business transaction and very professionally – you get what you paid for. For South Americans, moving people into North America is a challenge, a battle of wits between them and the border guards, with the occasional personal element as smugglers and guards get to know each other. In Europe, there is none of this. Smugglers do not care about who they smuggle – all they want is their money. There is no professional pride in this for them, just the hard reality of cash, death or imprisonment. There is no element of romance or excitement to their business. This reveals perhaps the starkest truth of the business – stripped to its bone, it's about money.

Looking at Europe as a homogenous area regarding immigration is not very helpful. It is more usefully divided into the east, consisting of Russia and the former USSR countries, and the west, made up of the EU members. Within the east and the west, both areas have traditionally had relatively open borders which make them excellent territory for smuggling people – and there are plenty there who wish to make a profit from human trafficking.

The collapse of the Soviet Union in 1991 stunned the world. While many were wishing to herald a new era of peace, there were others looking to profit and these groups were helped along by the West's inaction to fund Russia properly into the blossoming of a full democracy. Within years, many of the old Soviet states (also known as the Commonwealth of the Independent States (CIS) member countries) – some of which had been critical of the maintaining of the empire – had declared themselves independent, and millions of people who had once been citizens of the USSR were now Ukrainians and many other nationalities.

We have already seen one way in which East European smugglers operate – by trading on the dreams of women and enslaving them – but there are other ways. Many people willingly seek out the people smugglers so they can go elsewhere.

More than 100,000 people try to leave Russia and the CIS-member countries every year. Many more would like to try but money is a very big stumbling block where the average wage is less than what most Westerners spend in a week. Passage from Moscow to a EU country could cost between US$9,600 and US$14,460.

Most aim for Western Europe or the USA, which accept more than 10,000 legal immigrants a year. But some from the ex-Soviet states, despite enmity with 'Mother Russia', end up there permanently. Some are workers who were stranded there after the USSR divide; others looked at their homelands and decided they were better off in Russia.

But Russia is already overcrowded with immigrants. The then Russian Deputy Interior Minister Vladimir Vasiliyev claimed in 2001 that there were 10 million illegal immigrants in the country, half of whom were from former

USSR territories. According to Vasiliyev, the others were Chinese, who cross into Russia and stay in the area known as Primorye. The Chinese often enter with forged or expired Soviet passports and then use the black market to get genuine documents for US$1,000. Some then go on further west.

Other illegals in Russia include people who came to Russia for an education from the CIS-member countries and decided to stay. In addition, there are half a million legal immigrants who had work permits or other legal reasons to be there.

Another main problem for Russia is the agreements on visa-free entry concluded between the former Soviet republics and other countries including China, Iran and Pakistan. Vasiliyev was also worried about the emigration pattern in Russia. He claimed that, in 2000, just over 100,000 Russians left Russia for European countries. In particular, 56 per cent of them went to Germany, 23 per cent to Israel and 7 per cent to the United States.

But the situation goes both ways. Just as there are CIS citizens in Russia, there are Russians trapped in the CIS, trying to get home. Soviet estimates claim there could still be up to 20 million people trying to get back to loved ones. While the Kremlin says these potential immigrants would help to offset Russia's negative population growth, bureaucratic delays are stopping them from moving to Russia because there is a five-year backlog on waiting lists in some CIS countries. It's not just a case of turning up and having a card stamped.

Back in Russia, illegal immigrants were tolerated for a wide number of reasons. First, they were cheap labour. While this sometimes caused tension between immigrants and unemployed locals, police very often did not trouble people for ID papers. On a more political level, it was also recognised that a lot of these immigrants were sending money back to impoverished CIS countries, which was helping to make the difference between families starving and being fed. Wise politicians realised that lack of food and money would mean families going hungry and that could increase political instability. People with food in their bellies were less likely to revolt and that would – in its own small way – help keep the peace.

Things changed in 2002 when a group of Chechens held hostage 750 people in a Moscow cinema, in an attempt to force Russia to stop the war in Chechnya and withdraw 85,000 troops from there. The reaction this prompted is similar in some aspects to the way that some Middle-Eastern citizens were treated after the 11 September 2001 tragedy in the USA – foreigners were suddenly a target and there was an increase in racially motivated attacks in Russia's capital, leading to an increase in the number of people trying to leave.

Regardless of why they want to leave, when they do, Russians go to see people like Piotr. He had a general reluctance to reveal anything about himself to me, but he was willing to reveal plenty about smuggling operations for a fee. So perhaps he was one of the smugglers.

With his small, stocky build and dark hair, all Piotr needed was a long coat and Cossack hat to look like a stereotypical KGB officer drawn from the books of Le Carré or Fleming. 'The hardest thing about leaving Russia,' he boomed in a deep bass voice, 'is distance. You would have to go out of your way or be stupid to be caught but it does mean a lot of travelling.'

His reassuring tone is polished – like that of a salesman – and he later admits that, yes, there is some risk, 'but not a lot.' The key to it, he claims, is planning. 'Moving people willingly is not that hard. You are not having to threaten them and you are not being watched out for. The danger is if you are moving drugs, arms or something else – like caviar, believe it or not. Also, most of the guards are concentrating on the CIS borders with Afghanistan and China. Going west immediately increases your chances of getting away as there are so few guards.'

Getting into Poland is a matter of knowing who is on duty and having the right paperwork on you – US dollars being the best kind. 'Going across Poland makes things a lot cheaper for everyone concerned,' claims Piotr. 'For a start the car can have other things in it that may be of use to people in the West, which brings down the cost a little.

'The best smugglers have people who know the guards and, when they get to the border, they will be asked for paperwork and passports. Before approaching the border, anyone wanting to get in should have put US$10 or US$20 in their passport, depending on what is being carried. The passport is then returned without the money, the car moves on and everyone is happy, especially the guard who gets some money and doesn't have the hassle of having to search a vehicle.

'This practice is widespread. More cars than not every day will be carrying something that they shouldn't be – a person, guns, drugs, something. As I say, though, people are the easiest to get through as the other things can attract other agencies out with the normal border patrol. You don't want that.'

Such a system is clearly open to abuse, but Piotr claims that on at least one level, the border guards are fair. 'They will not detain someone because they have been paid to. There used to be tales of competitors bribing the guards to catch someone – and their haul – as a way of removing them, but all that ever happened was the guards ended up with money from both sides as the caught person would just bribe their way out of it.

'It got ridiculous as tit-for-tats were sparked off – and there was enough traffic congestion at borders without any more, which was what was happening with all these smuggler stoppages. Non-smugglers should be grateful this happens. If every car and truck was stopped then it would take a lot longer to cross the border.'

Of course, if all the cash was staying with the border guards, they wouldn't hang around for long and would all be sunning it in warmer climes than Poland, Belarus and Russia. What makes the smuggling at the Russian border so interesting is that it is a multi-layered system. Yes, the guard takes some of the money, but the rest goes up the chain of command. This is beneficial in a number of ways. First, it allows the smugglers to be tipped off when any 'outsider' official is at the border, carrying out an impromptu investigation. Second, the officials can tell their superiors that smuggling is not a problem in their sector. Third, the bosses pick the men under them, so they pick people who will continue to maintain the status quo. They do not pick idealistic people who want to change the system.

According to Piotr, the Western world has only itself to blame: 'You spend years telling us how good capitalism is and then don't expect us to use it to the logical end? Capitalism says money talks and that's all this proves.'

Of course, going this way is relatively more expensive than the other routes as it pretty much guarantees getting there. According to Piotr, it's the best way, but he knows of others, including the most dangerous route of all – through the site of the world's most deadly nuclear breakdown, Chernobyl. 'Fools,' says Piotr, with no sound of pity in his voice. 'Yes, it may be cheaper for them, but in the long term it costs them a lot more.'

Even more bizarre is the fact that the Russian authorities have seen cases of people moving through the still-irradiated zone and deciding to stay there, working on the theory that the law will never chase them there. Some of them even end up working for the drug dealers who grow large, occasionally mutated crops of marijuana and poppy in the zone. The area itself is more or less abandoned with villages smothered by grass and trees – perfect for hiding or starting a new life.

The area is so popular that there are now special border guards near Chernobyl, who are paid a larger sum than normal guards to patrol the area. However, there are even some areas that the guards – on their US$50 a month wage – will not patrol, and the smugglers know this, passing easily through the barbed wire that is meant to deter them.

According to Piotr, 'There are tales of small communities springing up around the drug activities. It is incredible, but I do not think they would ever pose a threat to anyone, given the radiation.'

The last kind of immigration that Piotr claims to know of ('Many people have nothing to do with the Chinese coming here. They organise that themselves, though some people "assist" them when they are in Russia') is something that is unique to Russia just now – but is a problem that Europe will have to face in decades to come.

'A lot of people being moved from the CIS states to Russia are not what you would call young. Quite the opposite, because the retirement age is lower in Russia than it is elsewhere in the CIS.' This is true in areas such as

Kazakhstan, which has retirement ages of three years higher than Russia.

'Kazakhstan is perhaps the most doomed place there is. The old want out and the young are fleeing because there is no education for them. The Government's hard-line nationalist policies are also driving away anyone who listens with their head and not their heart.'

The smugglers normally hand the refugees who go to the West over to local agents – or leave them to fend for themselves. But while it may be the West in geographical terms, it is run by the East. Most of the ganglords of western European (ie France, Germany etc) smuggling are from countries such as Romania, Estonia and other eastern European countries. This includes Russia, it has to be said. However, although their influence is weak on the UK mainland, in Europe their rule is absolute.

In a cafe in Vlora, South Albania, one smuggler told me why things were so easy for them. 'The authorities cannot keep up,' he said. 'We are better resourced, more intelligent and better financed. We charge a lot but most of that goes elsewhere to other people, like the police who operate the dockside barriers and security guards in the ports. Also, the cost of our equipment is not cheap.

'The best way to leave here is through Italy. You get there by ferry and then afterwards use the lorry network to travel to the channel ports. Depending on what you pay, you can travel risky routes or go by safer routes. The more money we get, the more we can bribe people along the routes. Our prices start at £700 and go up a lot.

'The Italians are a problem, though. They are putting up their guard more, with more boats and patrols, but most good speedboats can still get by them and if you use boys to ferry people across there is no danger of arrest, as the Italians will not arrest children. The only time this is a problem is when weather is bad as the children do not have experience of handing boats in stormy waters, but when weather is good using children is a great idea. They do not want as much money as adults; they gain good experience and people get abroad and, if they are caught, police do not arrest them. Everyone wins.

'We tell people wanting the UK that our route is best. We get them passports here, take them across the Adriatic by speedboat, then from southern Italy to Milan by lorry. There an associate of ours advises on transport to England, depending on what they can afford – and it can range from plane flights to hiding under freight trains. We also have French fishermen who for a bit of cash will take people across the English Channel.'

There are many ways to cross Europe as we have seen in previous chapters. Every country has its main operators who keep many of the immigrants in servitude until they have repaid their travel and smuggling debts; some have people work as sex slaves.

In Western Europe, being one large landmass, it is easy to see how people can move around with little difficulty or fear of being captured. What also helps is the Schengen Agreement, which allows free movement across most countries of mainland Europe, without border controls or checks. This is obviously a boon to smugglers: having managed to enter Germany, for example, their only concern is avoiding police.

For those wishing to reach Britain though, there is one more obstacle – the English Channel. In years gone by, the only way to cross was on ferries and by hiding in trucks – very few flew – but now, the Channel Tunnel gives many what they think is an easy way to sneak into Britain.

And in France, all too many people are willing to help them. Even a number of French taxi drivers are in on it. One driver I spoke to – who later helped me meet smugglers – was of the opinion: 'It is better to have them in your country than ours. This is nothing personal, we just don't want them. I personally have helped take hundreds of people to near the tunnel. You see a number of them a few times because in order to earn the chance to get through the tunnel, they have to help three or four other groups go before them.

'Some people run through as decoys, getting caught deliberately while others sneak by. Some tamper with equipment or try to stop the trains for a few moments. We take them out of Sangatte [the now closed Red Cross refugee camp] and drive them there. Some we even drive back before the authorities have noticed that they are missing.'

Some people resort to more desperate and expensive tactics. In 2002 the *Daily Mail* revealed that small-plane business flights are not always checked as thoroughly as commercial flights for immigrants and there are fears that plane-chartering is the smuggling method of the future. According to the *Mail*, one group of people tried it in late 2002. The group had to spend a month bringing their plan together, starting in Afghanistan where they had purchased fake passports. From there they went to Tajikistan and Uzbekistan, and then Moscow after getting fake visas arranged. Next a small travel firm called Aerotrans received a booking for the hire of an aircraft to take a group of people to Heathrow and the flight took place a few days later. When the plane landed in the UK and their documents were being examined, they claimed asylum.

For people in Britain terrified that their 'green and pleasant land' is being overrun with foreigners, there is one
hope, according to a number of smugglers I spoke to. Pascal
(who claimed to 'run with the smugglers') said: 'While
getting to Europe is not too tricky, it is still an effort to get
into the UK, even if you have associates in the UK like we
do. It is very hard to bribe your guards or police – either
that or we do not offer enough. The best way to get in just
now is to throw a lot of people at the place every night and
hope a number get through. They always will because you
can't catch everybody every night.

'Also, many of the ones you catch are held in camps with
other people, where they learn how better to avoid detec-
tion next time. It's like putting an innocent in with
criminals – they learn the tricks. The people in the camps –
which are in the UK – also have the chance to escape in
their chosen country. Some groups I know use that as a
plan – getting caught once actually in the UK. Why?
Because they will be fed and clothed and get a rest. Once
rested, they can try to escape.'

PART 3

THE AUTHORITIES

10

HUNDREDS OF MILES AND JUST ONE GUN: KEEPING AMERICA AMERICAN

America has always had a reputation for being a lawless land, from the days of the Wild Wild West to more recent fears over snipers and crazed celebrities. But just as there have always been lawbreakers, there have always been law enforcers. It is on the borders that the image of the old American West still thrives, we picture lone agent of the US Border Patrol standing at sunset, looking across to Mexico, making sure no one else sneaks into the country, adding to the millions already there.

That is the myth, the romantic image. The reality is considerably different. Over the last decade, America's borders have gone through an amazing transformation – from prairie deserts to the forefront of Fortress America.

It was around 1993 that new reforms were announced to deal with the rising problem of immigration, which was increasingly becoming a political matter. The plan was known as 'prevention through deterrence'; the aim, to make it so risky and dangerous that there would be no point in trying to sneak into America. In that sense, the plan was a failure. More than 3 million people still try to pour in from the south every year.

What it did was to 'militarise' the border line through a number of operations. These included what were known as Operation Gatekeeper in San Diego, Operation Hold the

Line in El Paso, Operation Rio Grande in McAllen and Operation Safeguard in Tucson. Operation Gatekeeper was the first and appeared to prove that deterrence worked. Initially, it concentrated on five miles of Imperial Beach – an area that accounted for nearly 25 per cent of all illegal border crossings nationwide. Once the border patrol regained control of this heavily trafficked stretch, Gatekeeper was expanded to include the entire 66 miles of border under the San Diego sector's jurisdiction.

As a result, apprehensions in 2001 reached a 28-year low in the sector, a reduction from 45 per cent of all apprehensions nationwide before Gatekeeper to only 9 per cent. One sign of the success is that smuggling costs to go this way have risen phenomenally, from US$250 per person to as much as US$1,500.

Operation Hold the Line was next, being implemented in the El Paso area in 1993. This produced a 50 per cent decline in apprehensions between 1993 and 1996. Then in 1995 the controversial Operation Safeguard was launched. This plan redirected illegal border crossings away from urban areas to comparatively open areas that the border patrol could control more effectively, especially when there were more than 1,100 agents patrolling the area – a fourfold increase from when the operation was launched.

After that, Operation Rio Grande gained control of the border in the Rio Grande Valley and then in all of Texas and New Mexico. This saw a massive influx of new border patrol agents – almost 500, which was a 50 per cent increase on previous years' staffing – and they got results. In some areas immigration flow appeared to fall by at least one third. Crime in cities close to the border also appeared to drop considerably.

Much technology has been put in place, allowing agents to cover larger areas more efficiently. This includes low-light surveillance cameras, miles of border lighting and lights that are triggered only when someone trips an infra-red beam, among other things.

Old-fashioned tactics, including the building of 14-foot concrete walls and fences, are also used, not so much to try and deter people – though that is an aim – but more to stop vehicles getting through. The idea is that by setting up more permanent presences near the fences and walls, people will be put off from crossing nearby and try somewhere else. The theory also states that people may eventually give up if there is no easier place at which to cross.

Critics point out that Safeguard, more than any other of the schemes, forces people to use more dangerous routes to try to enter the country. The response is that if it is dangerous, people should not make the attempt and, besides, that the scheme should act as a deterrent is the whole point in the first place. Patrols are not there to help immigrants across.

Agents say that the new system is not successful at deterrence. People keep trying, regardless of the risk, as they think they will get through. They are too blinded by the American dream to realise the border reality.

Older agents find the new rulebook quite mystifying at times. They can no longer take whatever action they want to apprehend illegal crossers. They are told to remain in a particular area, what illegal traffic they are to pursue and how far they can go, as well as being accountable for their whereabouts at all times.

Many agents dislike the new methods. Some find their new duties boring while others believe the new strategy is ineffective. Numerous agents believed that Gatekeeper was more about politics than actually about catching immigrants. Agents began talking about their suspicions, and word of alleged number-fixing to make the operations look good began to spread. But both the Clinton and the Bush administrations continued to support the figures, which show that in total more than 1 million people were being caught every year.

But now, people are starting to ask what should be done next, as the annual number of border patrol arrests remains fairly constant. In 1995, for example, 1.2 million illegal aliens were apprehended, then 1.5 million in 1996, 1.4 million in 1997, 1.5 million in 1998, 1.5 million in 1999, 1.6 million in 2000, 1.2 million in 2001 and 1.1 million in 2002. Agents and politicians are now calling for reforms to improve things.

There have been calls for the National Guard and Army to become involved, but the border patrol agents say this is not necessary. What they want is to be allowed to do their job.

Mark has been in the border patrol service for almost 15 years. While it's a decent life, he claims it's nothing like the romanticised myth, 'Now, it's a lot more like being a desk clerk of some kind. Don't get me wrong. I'm not saying that in days gone by there was more of wild chasing, lasting hours, across deserts and so on, but there was some of that and it did make the job more exciting.

'You felt as if you were out there making a difference, catching drug smugglers and putting people back into Mexico. Now, you only get out when you are on a rota for it. The worrying thing is that there are many agents who now just want to sit in and watch the cameras, sending others they like to "sitting on X", which is the phrase we use now. It means you're just sitting on a point on a map; not actually out there, chasing the smugglers or the aliens.'

'Out there' is a phrase used a lot by the older agents, who lament what has happened. At any time, at least 2,000 agents are 'working the line', as it is known, but not all of them – in fact sometimes not even most of them – are out, driving about, looking for smugglers or illegal immigrants. When I spent some time with the border patrol, I seemed to find glorified accountants – which is unsurprising to an extent, as college-level entrants are on the rise.

Since 1995, the percentage of border patrol recruits with bachelor degrees has risen from 30 per cent to 40 per cent. At the same time, those with military experience decreased from 47 per cent to 37 per cent. For those new agents, the minimum annual salary will be about US$30,400, including mandatory overtime. After six months, successful agents move up a pay grade to about US$42,500 per year, including overtime. With overtime, experienced agents can easily make more than US$50,000 a year.

There is still some excitement to the job but, as another agent pointed out, not as much as before: 'The work is still there, but we have more restraints on us that make it harder to do the same job. It's taken a lot of the satisfaction out of the job. We now have a very narrow area of responsibility. For example, we used to patrol five miles of the border. Bosses would say that you were free to chase anyone who came on your patch – and you could chase them until you caught 'em. But now you're lucky if your patrol takes in more than 300 yards of the border and it takes a great deal of approval from people to give pursuit.

'Also, now we're expected to accept temporary assignments of a month or more away from home as well as assignments that could be anywhere along the Mexican border. In days gone by there was more respect and you felt you were treated like professionals. Now, everyone seems to be an expert on our job without knowing a goddamn thing.'

Mark is fairly sanguine about his job. He accepts why people are trying to enter the USA – 'When you have a Third World economy next to a First World economic power, you will always have this problem or people wanting to be here. It's understandable' – and, while the job is not what it used to be, it still has moments for him. 'I'm lucky. I've never had to fire at someone, but I know agents who have. People smuggling is still on the rise. Drug smuggling is what the emphasis is on for us. The walls and so on are meant to keep the people out.

'The things some people try to get in can be funny – sad but funny. I remember one vehicle where a man had been put into a car seat, and they had actually done a good job of it, but in order to make it look authentic, they had decided to have someone sit on him for the journey. They get to the border and the vehicle is about to be nodded through when the passenger breaks wind very loudly and, it has to be said, it's smelly.

'The chair then starts bulging in parts as the man hidden in the seat tries to hit the man on the seat for breaking wind. It actually had a serious side as the man who had been sewn in was throwing up. If we hadn't got him out, he probably would have choked.

'Situations rarely got violent, but that is on the increase as people get more and more desperate to get into the USA or to avoid getting caught, and there have been deaths recently. We are not kidding ourselves about the fact that this can still be a dangerous job.

'You do still get funny moments, but there's less of the drama of big chases across miles of land with people shooting at you. They were fairly dramatic, and I'd be a liar if I didn't say fun, but it was only fun if we got the guys and none of us were injured.'

At one stage, things were so bad that Mark left the service to try to patch things up with his wife. ('At first she thought it was cool that she was going with a border agent. A lot of girls find it cool at first but that wears off as the reality sets in.') She was disenchanted with rarely seeing her husband, but after they separated, Mark reapplied and returned to the border patrol.

'They even sent me to the academy again – it was ridiculous. I had more experience than most of the instructors and the new sector I was put in had a section chief with only four years' experience, which is nothing. When I started, a boss had at least 15 years in. Now it's people with no experience running the show.

'To an extent that suits the penpushers because they don't want people who are restless about sitting around, waiting for action, and that's what most of the long-timers are. Of course, there are fewer of them about, as everyone is going to jobs with better pay and more excitement.'

One of the more popular choices for border agents is to become air marshals (performing armed security and other functions on planes), where salaries, which are based on the applicant's experience and background, can be as high as US$80,000. In fact, one of the few good things about being in the service at the moment is that it leads to better jobs. More than 25 per cent of the border patrol staff have said they are unhappy in their job and many of them are so unhappy they want to leave. They are so demotivated, they do only the bare minimum for their job. It is now at the stage that the bosses are concerned.

'We're spending over US$50,000 to train these individuals to be border patrol agents, and then they're leaving – why?'

said Ron Sanders, former chief of the border patrol's Tucson sector.

So many are leaving that it is becoming impossible to meet Washington's demands for 1,000 new agents every year. The average net annual gain over the last few years has been nearer 400, because of the number of people retiring or moving on. As mentioned above, there have been calls for the National Guard and Army to help.

I visited Douglas, Arizona, a small town on the Mexican border. Unusually, one agent I spoke to there agreed: 'There is another problem. We obviously chase drug smugglers and a lot of times now the drug smugglers are getting in on the people-smuggling racket. This becomes a problem when you look at the help the drug dealers have in the form of corrupt Mexican military officers and police officials.

'These guys are paid well. We've heard that more than US$500 million is spent by the Mexicans on bribes and some of these people have no fears about doing anything they have to, to keep the money coming.'

Border patrol agents in Douglas were once pulled from their duty stations after police in Aqua Prieta, Mexico, tipped off US authorities about a pending drug shipment. Supervisors were fearful of putting their agents in the middle of a shoot-out between rival smuggling gangs, each supported by competing Aqua Prieta police.

Official figures show that there have been at least 30 or 40 excursions – or 'mistakes' as the official diplomatic line goes – on to US land by the Mexican military, some of which resulted in unprovoked shootings.

The agent added: 'I've seen them come across the border, heavily armed and equipped, and I often wonder why we're not doing anything about it. We are told not to provoke them, but I'm sorry, someone crossing the border into my country and being heavily armed is very provocative.'

A number of situations have been recorded, including ones in 2000 where Mexican army soldiers have shot at guards in vehicles and also at border patrol helicopters. One of the most terrifying happened in May 2002 when an agent was fired on by three Mexican soldiers in a military Humvee near what is known as the San Miguel gate on the Tohono reservation, about 30 miles north-west of Nogales, Arizona.

The gunfire shattered the rear window of the US agent's four-wheel-drive vehicle. One bullet was deflected by the vehicle's prisoner partition, located directly behind the agent's seat. It then knocked out the right rear window. The agent involved had been on the job for about a year, authorities said.

Despite complaints about these incidents, little is ever done. And the risk of border work does not affect just border agents. Residents of nearby towns get caught up in passing events or have their homes broken into. National Park staff can also be at risk.

In August 2002, Service Ranger Kris Eggle was shot in the Organ Pipe Cactus National Monument in Arizona, from over the border – allegedly by Mexican officers chasing a man hiding in bushes. There was never any official inquiry and who shot Mr Eggle remains a mystery that will probably never be solved, though many have their suspicions.

Colorado politician Tom Tancredo is calling for change. He said: 'There's no doubt Mexican military units along the border are being controlled by the cartels, and not by Mexico City. The military units operate freely, with little or no direction, and several of them have made numerous incursions into the United States.

'Mexican President Vicente Fox may be trying to take control of his military, but there is a major disconnect between him and them – particularly among the units along the USA–Mexico border.'

To some agents, it is obvious why the Mexicans shoot. One said: 'It may not even be about killing us, but if they can take out a vehicle or injure someone, then that is a person or vehicle that cannot be patrolling the border trying to keep people and drugs out, so perhaps having our Army here would help. It would certainly send a message.'

Agents like Mark and Jon do not think that's necessary. According to Jon, 'People will always keep coming and the way to improve things would be to do things like letting the agents get out there more. Assign the older staff or the physically incapable ones to the X posts and let the rest of us get out there, going to places when needed and roaming the rest of the time. Also, let us give pursuit without asking for permission. At the moment we are technically meant to wait for the go-ahead before chasing.

'But there has to be more to it than just empowering us. You have to start looking at the reasons people come here. They come here because of jobs, so why not punish the people who employ them?'

Jon wants to see more US Government intervention: 'And America has to stop bending over backwards to try and help them out. We have immigration cards and amnesties that sure don't help us do our job. I voted for Bush as I thought he would tighten things up – he's done the opposite.

'Politicians hate to get involved, because they see aliens as useful. Republicans look at them as a source of would-be cheap workers, while Democrats view them as potential voters, so everybody's using them – from the people who smuggle them to the Government.'

This last point is very real. As well as in working in the United States, immigrants have to pay for food, housing and many other services and products. It has been estimated that at least US$140 billion of the American economy now comes from illegal aliens – mostly Asians and Mexicans. In the late twentieth century, immigrants increased the work-force growth from 11 per cent in the 1970s to nearly one-third in the 1990s. It has been suggested that, just as it did decades ago, America thrives now only because of the underclass of immigrants willing to do the jobs that no one else will for wages that others would find insulting.

Koreans own about 29 per cent of food stores, Chinese own about 54 per cent of Asian restaurants and Vietnamese own 27 per cent of the nail-care salons. Asian-Indians own about 17,000 hotels and motels. Mexicans tend to take the jobs that no one else wants. However, the financial benefits have to be offset by the costs of illegal immigrants. Billions are spent on their health care, but one of the biggest costs is the budget for border guards. And they are trying to recruit still more.

But, as Mark puts it, they should at least know what they are getting into, 'They keep advertising this job as defend-ing the American dream, playing on the old-style romance and excitement of the job. The reality is very different and people should realise that.'

The agents' task is not a popular one. They are obviously not popular with the Mexicans, but they are also now falling out of favour with Americans who live near the border. For example, as policy has shifted from capture to deterrence, people who live on the border do not feel as safe. According to Pia Adams, who lives in a small town near Douglas: 'The young guards now don't have a clue and I'd hate to have to rely on them in an emergency. There are times when they have stopped me to ask for directions.

'Also, I've heard tales of people calling them, saying that there's an alien sneaking about, and they haven't responded because it's just one person and it doesn't look as good on their results as catching a group of ten. The thing is, they need us. Not only are they our neighbours and so on, but if they don't help us when we need them why should we help them in any way? If they won't make the effort for us, why should we do it for them?'

In Douglas itself, some people feel the border patrol agents are more of a problem than the aliens. 'Twenty-four hours a day they are about and they seem to have no respect for local people. They are among the noisiest people ever known here and they've woken up many a child or adult by slamming car doors, shouting loudly and so on,' said Douglas resident Mary Tatlin.

While residents of many towns along the border may have problems with the patrol agents, there are also others who feel the current policy is not proactive enough and go out to do the job themselves. Groups such as the American Border Patrol (ABP) scour the countryside at the border. The ABP is a recently established, non-profit, Arizona corporation that, with the help of local volunteers, hopes to draw attention to the illegal activities along the border, by going through the towns as well as the desert hunting for immigrants. It has gained a lot of support and even has two former US Border Patrol officials serving on its board of directors. People from all walks of life join these groups, including people with military backgrounds, ex-border agents and armed civilians. The official line is that they are doing what Americans throughout history have done – doing the job themselves because no one else will do it.

ABP member Bill King, who was once the border patrol's chief agent, said the situation is the worst he's seen in 45 years. He claims it is because some of the weakest people at the top of the Government agency are coming up with the wrong ideas for the dedicated field agents.

The group claims to obey the law and help illegal immigrants by providing them with water and food. What the members do not do is to let illegal immigrants continue their trek north into the United States. Glenn Spencer, executive director of the US Border Patrol, told me, 'Instead, they call on the US Border Patrol to pick them up and send them south,' he said.

Roger Barnett has been associated with the ABP. He and his brother Don are legendary characters, renowned for getting out there and doing it, living proof that the values that made America great still exist. In 2002 Roger and Don detected and reported almost 2,500 immigrants to the border patrol – more than in previous years, which is why they scorn claims that the number of people trying to get into America is stabilising.

Barnett has some controversial ideas but, at the same time, he has struck a chord with his Douglas neighbours. More than 100 people go out in groups across the border. Many others help him with information or details. What he does is find would-be immigrants and then force them back to the border or, if he runs into a group of border agents, he'll hand them over to them. He has made enemies though – on both sides of the border. In Mexico, there is a US$10,000 bounty on his head, while in the USA critics claim that he has the help of the Ku Klux Klan – something he strongly denies, saying he doesn't need their help as there are plenty of other volunteers.

He feels one way to end the immigration problem would be to make everyone American. 'A lot of people say that the United States needs to invade Mexico. I think that's a hell of an idea. There's a lot of mines and great beaches there, there's farming and resources. Think of what the USA could do there and then Mexicans wouldn't have to come up here any more. It's an invasion. Like someone said, it's a slow-moving invasion, one or two miles an hour, but it's an invasion.'

Unsurprisingly, he has a lot of support in Douglas. One man, Marty, who claims to go on patrols with Barnett, said: 'We need to show them that they are not wanted and they cannot come here, cause hell and then take our money and jobs. I quite honestly believe that there should be hunting on the aliens with a bounty for everyone captured. We also have the right to defend ourselves but many people are scared just now. That will not last.'

Other people are also taking matters into their own hands. In the Otay Mesa area, Muriel Watson is organising vehicle blockades along the border, with more than 100 cars turning on their lights at night to deter anyone trying to sneak across. Ms Watson's plan is for a wall to be built in her area. 'There's nothing here, because the Government wimps out when the Mexicans complain that a Berlin-type wall is being built, which is nonsense. We just want to feel safe. I feel something should be done. Our vehicular protest is our way of bringing attention to it.'

The US Border Patrol regards the other groups as both a help and a hindrance. 'They mean well, but they can get in the road and, God forbid, if there was a fatality, that would open up a complete minefield, regardless of the dead person being American or Mexican. If it was an American, there would be outrage that we weren't out there doing our job. A lot of border agents would agree with that sentiment because, remember, we don't make the policy. A lot of us don't like it, we just have to follow it.

'If it was a Mexican fatality, there's a whole new situation. You could be in a position where you had to arrest an American who thinks he's done nothing wrong. There's also the possibility of revenge attacks. The more liberal sections of the media would have a go at us for letting it happen.'

Borders and divisions exist not only on maps and in landscapes, they can also exist in the mind. America seems truly divided about the problem. It cannot work out whether immigrants are useful or a burden. Unless it decides the former, America may well remain a land of borders and not the land of the free.

11

A TUNNEL FULL OF TROUBLE:
WESTERN EUROPE'S DILEMMA

The task of guarding Europe from the scourge of illegal people smuggling is quite different to the US. Europe – with the exception of former war zones such as Bosnia – deals with the matter in a slightly more low-key manner by using police forces. Normally unarmed forces unless there is a terrorist risk.

Over recent years, there has been a massive rise in police funding in this area as it has moved from being a question of minor concern to a major issue, requiring a lot of human resources.

To the credit of European forces, much of the handling of the problem has been undertaken at a local level, only calling in the resources of Interpol or information from the UN or even MI5 and MI6 when it is absolutely necessary. The UN – apart from its peacekeeper role in war zones – can do little, but through its agencies, it can excel at information gathering. For example, the UN information agency IRIN was able to tip off authorities about an immense upcoming influx in smuggled Somalian children.

A report in 2002 found that more than 250 children a month were being sneaked out of Somalia because of fighting among warlords and a rising number of child deaths due to famine, poor health or the actual fighting. Once they get to an airport, the smugglers leave most of the children, unless their parents have paid enough to see the child taken further. Some of the smugglers keep the children and raise them into lives of prostitution or crime.

According to an UN spokesman: 'Many of the smugglers were asked to try to get the children to Britain because it is believed to have an excellent welfare state and also because there is a large Somali community of over 70,000 people. When we heard what was happening, police forces and other agencies were able to react to it.'

One of these reactions was the introduction by the British embassy in Addis Ababa of compulsory DNA-testing for Somali asylum seekers, in a bid to stop children being hidden in families offered asylum. Another step was the alerting of officials to the passports being used. The smugglers were using genuine passports with valid numbers but, if they were run through the official computer system, no name would come up. As a Passport Office source revealed: 'It's a genuine passport in that the passport number and so on are valid. But the number itself has not been given to anyone. Essentially these people are using blank passports. They are very handy because they can be reused a number of times – until they are scanned – and then the game is given away.

'Think of it like a car without an owner – it has a registration plate, but no owner. The passport has a number, but no legal or official owner. It has been made but it is in theory, blank and, while the crooks may put pictures on them, when this passport is scanned through the system, the computer will reveal that it hasn't actually been issued formally yet. This process starts with an inside job and that's something we are trying to clamp down on.'

Details like these, along with information on smuggler movements, have helped the police to make a number of arrests.

Interpol has also been helpful in the gathering and sharing of information. In June 1999, upon the request of member states, Interpol General Secretariat initiated Project Bridge to facilitate a more effective and efficient programme for the collection of information on organised crime groups and associations involved in alien-smuggling, for improving combat of this crime and for undertaking adequate measures on the levels of prevention and investigation. It appears to have been working, allowing for courts across Europe to prosecute more and more people smugglers as police share knowledge.

As one Interpol officer said: 'Sharing the knowledge is important – as is sharing the praise – because there have been times in the past when various countries have been accused of not doing much because the praise will only go to the country which made the arrest. This often meant that, for example, if the Italians missed their chance to catch a smuggler, they wouldn't tell others of where they were going as there was nothing in it for them. Now, if the French just miss a capture of smugglers going to England, quite often they will tip off the English authorities. The English will catch them but the operation will be praised as a joint Anglo-French operation.'

It was also Interpol that revealed in 2001 that smugglers were reusing the old trick of getting birth certificates for dead babies and using them to gain passports. This led to the development of a system known as the Events Linkage Verification System – or Elvis. It works by linking death records with birth records. Running this data against passport records pinpoints passports that have been issued in a dead person's name.

At the start of 2003, five European Union countries launched a joint maritime surveillance scheme, in order to stop illegal immigrants arriving in Europe by sea. The pilot project, called Operation Ulysses, is coordinated by Spain together with Britain, France, Portugal and Italy. This joint operation is a step closer to a European-wide frontier police force.

There are Franco-German plans for a EU police force that would fight against trafficking and control the flow of migrants. At the end of 2002 UK authorities announced the Crime (International Cooperation) Bill, which would allow foreign police to operate on British soil if they were in pursuit of a criminal. This also allows British police the same rights in other European Union countries, though there is an exception for Britain's police forces in Ireland.

But police are not sure about these plans. Speaking about people smuggling and increases in sentencing from seven to ten years in the UK, alongside £2,000 fines for lorry drivers for every smuggled immigrant, National Crime Intelligence Service (NCIS) director-general John Abbott said, 'I would be surprised if they had a significant impact. They [illegal immigrants] pay up to £20,000 each and some believe they can enter the country legally. Once they arrive they find themselves forced into prostitution or petty crime or working in restaurants to pay off their debts to the smugglers. The indications are that despite actions being taken, the market will increase and profits will remain high.'

Roy Penrose, head of the National Crime Squad, backed this up, saying: 'Professional traffickers have found a very lucrative commodity in the form of immigrants. I don't see the trade abating.'

But the rise in smuggling has been accompanied by a rise in information gathering and the number of arrests and prosecutions, as authorities try to deter people from getting involved. As one Interpol member put it, 'It's really hard to get at the heads of the organisations – mostly because of where they are based and because people close to them are so loyal. But if we can strike at their local workers and have them too scared to work, then that might be the way to break them up or at least diminish their power incredibly.'

In recent years there have been a number of court cases that not only show that police efforts are rising in the battle but also reveal many of the tactics used by the smugglers. For example, a search by the French Frontier Police, the PAF, resulted in a number of smuggling accomplices being convicted, including a large number of taxi drivers who no one would suspect while driving into any area. One driver revealed to the French authorities how a gang of 12 preyed on asylum seekers at the Red Cross centre at Sangatte, near the Channel Tunnel entrance, charging them £700 each to try to sneak them aboard a train or lorry bound for Britain. The court also heard that traffickers target truck stops and lay-bys on the motorways and trunk roads leading to Calais and the other main channel ports – Dunkirk and Dieppe in France and Ostend in Belgium. Then, as drivers sleep in cabs or shop for bargains, gang leaders instruct refugees on how to break into trailers and hide for the perilous journey across the English Channel.

There have been other cases as France tries to clamp down on the problem. One group, referred to during their trial as 'the Kurds', specialised in packing stowaways on lorries passing through Calais, and on freight trains using the Channel Tunnel. A second group, dubbed 'the Algerians', ferried refugees to poorly supervised railway goods yards, far away from the tight security at the ports. They had contacts within the French national railway SNCF's freight division, who gave them precise information about which trains at which goods yard would be passing through the tunnel to Britain.

According to one PAF officer, current laws are a hindrance. 'We know who the traffickers are but we have no evidence to convict them as the laws are too strict on proof – the system favours the criminals. Whenever anyone is stopped in the whole of northern France and claims to be an asylum seeker heading for Britain they are automatically taken to Red Cross centres. Once they are there they are in the hands of the gangsters very often.'

Of course many of the centres are now closed, but in some areas the gangsters' influence remains and many asylum seekers will go to these areas to try and find help to be smuggled.

An ingenious way of moving people in the UK was discovered in 2001 when a removal firm was revealed to have been moving more than furniture. Forty-three-year-old Stephen Hobbs was jailed for nine years and his older brother 44-year-old John was sent down for a seven-and-a-half-year sentence after it was revealed that their firm, Hobbs Removals, travelled back and forth to mainland Europe loaded with illegal immigrants – many of whom had paid up to £10,000 a head for passage to the UK. Two others were also convicted in the case – Darren, John Hobbs' 25-year-old son, and Warren Charge, 29, both for three years. All were found guilty of conspiring to facilitate the illegal entry of immigrants into the country. The sentences for John and Stephen are among the highest handed out in the UK.

Canterbury Crown Court heard during the case that the brothers would board a ferry in Europe bound for Britain, and sit drinking coffee while their lorry was filled up with illegal immigrants. The operation during which John

Hobbs was arrested took place in 2000 when a lorry he was driving was opened to reveal 37 illegal immigrants. He was arrested, but later released after denying all knowledge of the refugees in the back of his truck.

Incredibly, despite his arrest, another trip was arranged. Darren Hobbs and Warren Charge drove two vehicles to Paris where they filled up wooden crates with illegal immigrants. On their return, John and Stephen Hobbs drove a third, empty vehicle as a decoy because they knew they were likely to be stopped. The ploy failed, however, and police at Dover found 59 people in the two lorries. It later emerged that the 96 immigrants – all men aged between 16 and 30 – had travelled from the Indian subcontinent.

In other European countries – particularly Belgium – there have been far fewer prosecutions. In some cases, this is because of the ages of people involved, as when Albanians use Italian children, but Spanish police officer Miguel Rancel gave another reason: 'There are prosecutions but many people here end up on trial by God because they are dead before they reach the courts. Not because of anything that happens to them once they reach custody, but because they choose perilous routes and die in the attempt to reach here.'

It is not only border guards, customs officers and politicians who are involved in the battle against people smuggling. Some of the most important work is carried out by people who can be a long distance away from the front line. Companies such as American Science and Engineering Inc. (AS&E) and Rapiscan are specialists in developing new methods to try to detect illegal immigrants at a time when, as we have seen, the tactics being used grow more surreptitious by the day.

AS&E have used a cutting-edge method known as backscatter technology – or X-ray lite – combined with traditional X-ray methods to produce superior images of what may be contained within luggage, crate containers or vehicles. Normal X-rays scan objects and present a surface image, but cannot always provide a detailed image of exactly what is being looked at. The backscatter X-ray makes use of rays bounced off an object rather than rays that pass through it, as in a traditional X-ray.

This technique shows up hidden immigrants and drugs because organic material bounces back more rays than inorganic matter. 'A backscatter image is like a photographic negative,' according to AS&E's chief technology officer Joseph Callerame. 'What you see is akin to what you would see if you were to peel back the door of a cargo container that is being surveyed.'

In June 2000, after the discovery of the dead Chinese immigrants at Dover, the UK Government placed a US$5 million order with AS&E for two mobile X-ray units. The scanners were installed in November 2000. Their locations have been kept secret, in order to keep smugglers on their toes, but insiders have commented on the usefulness of the system.

Another technology currently being developed is terahertz detectors which allow you to see through most things. It is a new area, with research being lead by groups in the Netherlands, notably Paul Planken at Delft Technical University, and by British company Teraview of Cambridge that may allow for even better findings in future. Terahertz rays are absorbed by water, but will pass a fair way through most dry substances including stone or sand.

12

IF THEY CAN'T LAND,
THEY CAN'T CLAIM ASYLUM:
HOW AUSTRALIA'S LEFT GOES FAR WHITE

Australia is defended in very different ways to America, Europe and other parts of the world. In fact, while Australia, like every other country, has immigration and customs officers who, along with law enforcement agencies, fight what they perceive to be the problem of illegal immigration, it would be fair to say that Australia is possibly one of the most aggressive first-world countries when it comes to the pursuit and prevention of aliens reaching its shores. It uses a considerable amount of its naval fleet to hunt for illegal immigrant ships coming towards its waters. There is no waiting until the ships even get near shore. The minute they are spotted in Australian waters, they are targeted and taken back out to international seas.

The Australian Government won't give details of how many ships – and what types – are used in the pursuit of immigrants, but according to a Navy insider, most ships are used at some point or another. 'Going chasing after immigrant boats is now looked on as just another part of training, though calling it a "chase" is a bit misleading as there's no chase. You see them and you catch them. The CO will radio other boats to let them know – and so they keep their eyes open in case the boat we've found is a decoy.

'Of course once you get to them, you face a whole new set of problems – with them and with liberals and the media when you get back home. It's not even about the old "Australia was conquered by immigrants, so we should let more turn up" argument. To be honest, it's just dull and that's the biggest problem with it. That's why the claims by people that sometimes the immigrants get beaten up by the Navy boys is nonsense. They might get shoved about, but that's it. And normally that's to get them off their own falling-apart boats. Believe me, once you've been on one of those things, you don't hang about.

'Besides, we could never see what the problem was. We were either obeying orders or trying to help them. It's not like the Vietnamese Navy, who used to use boats with immigrants as target practice and sink the boats, killing people, but the way some people go on, you'd think we were as bad as them.'

The Australian Navy also uses planes to spot boats that might be full of immigrants, which is understandable as it allows for the rapid identification of boats and for Navy vessels to be sent to areas to head off illegal ships. Although some may find this a little too heavy handed, there is nothing too untoward about it.

Sending in the hard-core Australian Special Air Services (SAS) is another matter. But that's exactly what the Australian Government did in August 2001.

A Norwegian freighter, the *Tampa*, was in international seas near Australia when it received a distress message from Australian search and rescue agencies, asking if it could go to a ship that they had heard was sinking. The vessel's captain, Arne Rinnan, agreed to help and was guided to the spot by Australian coastal surveillance aircraft. There the leaking boat, which was holding mostly Afghanistani refugees, was discovered to be in a terrible condition.

Even though the *Tampa* was registered to take carry only around 50 people, Captain Rinnan got more than 450 refugees – including a number of women and children – on his boat to prevent them drowning. He then proceeded to set a course for Indonesia, but a considerable number of the refugees then threatened to jump overboard if the ship did not set sail for Australia. Captain Rinnan changed course, after getting assurances that he would be allowed to dock at Christmas Island. The situation seemed in hand until the Howard-led Government held an emergency meeting to declare that the ship would not be allowed to dock. In fact, the Government went as far as to suggest that, as it was a Norwegian ship, the problem was one for the Norwegians to sort out, so the immigrants should go there and the matter had nothing to do with Australia.

A stalemate broke out with the ship berthed four nautical miles from Christmas Island. By this time Indonesia had said it would not take the refugees. But Australia had also made it clear that it did not want them and was doing very little to resolve the situation, refusing requests for food, water, drugs or medical staff.

The ship's chief mate, Chris Maltau, recalled: 'As soon as they were told they had been refused entry by Australia the refugees all went on a hunger strike. They were refusing to accept any food, water and medicine.'

Only one person on board had medical training of any kind and he had to call his father – a qualified doctor back in Norway – for advice on a regular basis. After talking to him, it was determined that several asylum seekers were suffering from dehydration and heat stress, and could die. But the Australian Government did not blink. The ship's crew gave up their bedding for the refugees, but the Australians still did nothing, even though they knew everything that was happening because they were illegally tapping many of the calls to the ship.

Captain Rinnan then became extremely distressed about the situation. By now 15 refugees had collapsed, with three of them not responding to light, sound, water or any form of treatment, and two of them foaming at the mouth. So he put out a 'pan-pan' distress call, which is a serious matter and second only to a mayday call.

Meanwhile in Norway, people were amazed and disgusted at Australia's response to the situation. The seafaring nation could not understand it, as most problems involving ships in distress see the people in trouble rescued and dropped off at the nearest civilised land.

The popular image of Australia was destroyed practically overnight, with some newspapers comparing Howard's tactics to those of Margaret Thatcher in the Falklands in the early 1980s, saying both actions were clearly designed for one thing only: to win elections.

Wallenius Wilhelmsen, the shipping line the *Tampa* worked with, said the company was stunned by Australia's 'callous' actions, and they warned of legal action against the Australian Government if the *Tampa* was forced back into international waters.

At the same time, the Norwegian Government was protesting Australia's actions to the International Maritime Organisation, the United Nations and the International Red Cross. Foreign Minister Thorbjoern Jagland said the Howard Government's attitude was 'inhumane' and contravened international law. He said: 'Australian authorities appealed to *Tampa* to assist the refugees in distress, and led the freighter to the position of the sinking vessel. It was therefore unacceptable that Australia did not allow the ship to go to the nearest Australian harbour.'

It was not only Norway that remonstrated. 'This is not the way to handle a refugee situation,' thundered UN Secretary-General Kofi Annan.

But the Australian Government did not care what others thought. Foreign Minister Alexander Downer told ABC television's acclaimed show *Lateline*, 'I'm not going to talk about the mechanisms we'll use, but we'll certainly take it out of Australian territorial waters.' And Howard told reporters outside Parliament that 'That boat will never land in our waters – never!'

Meanwhile, the captain and his crew decided to take matters into their own hands, disgusted at Australia's breach of long-standing international conventions that permit ships in distress to go to the nearest safe harbour. As they approached Christmas Island, 'to take shelter to be able to effect transfer of medical assistance', as the captain later told reporters, Australia finally did something. Twelve hours after the pan-pan call went out, it sent in a squad of Australian SAS troops in full military gear and armed with automatic weapons to seize control of the *Tampa*. It was a move that took most of the world by surprise. No one praised them for it. The crack team were dispatched the second the boat entered Australian waters. It boarded, and ordered Captain Rinnan to take the boat back to international seas.

In an incredible act of bravery and morality, he refused, turning the engines off instead. At this point, things should have gone better for the refugees. The SAS had brought a medic with them, the local Government on Christmas Island had said it wanted the boat to dock for humanitarian reasons and under International Refugee Conventions the people on the boat had to be given the right to asylum because they were in a nation's waters and no longer in international seas. They were not given the chance.

Flouting international law and protocol left the Australian Government in a predicament so, to legalise their actions, they brought in a new, emergency bill – the Border Protection Bill – which would provide 'absolute discretion' to military officers or Government officials to detain and remove a ship from Australian waters and to force back on board anyone who left the ship. It stated that any refugee on such a vessel would be barred from applying for a refugee visa. It would also prevent legal challenges in any court to the actions of the Government or officials.

Fortunately, the bill was not passed, but a motion to put the *Tampa* back in international seas was. But while the politicians were arguing, *Tampa* staff and the SAS were spending hours trying to save the lives of people on the boat. Eventually a decision was reached. It started with the kindness of New Zealand, ashamed at the actions of its neighbour. New Zealand's Prime Minister Helen Clark made an offer for 150 of the refugees. The Australians managed to find a home for the rest – the island of Nauru, the world's smallest republic, via Papua New Guinea and Auckland.

Nauru wasn't their first choice. Officials in the Australian Government revealed to me that Fiji refused because of troubles between its indigenous and ethnic-Indian communities and Tuvalu also said 'No'. According to Australian insiders, this was felt to be payback for an appeal it made to Australia in 2001 for some islanders to go there as the Tuvalu Government was worried about rising sea levels.

While some seemed satisfied by this and the Howard Government thought it was no longer an issue, there was further outrage when the cost of the operation was revealed

The insider told me: 'The total bill was around A$40 million, which is about US$20 million. Taking them to a refugee centre and keeping them there for processing would have cost A$2 million at the very most. The problem – and for them it was a tragedy – was that once a stance had been taken, Howard would not back down. It's not in his nature and he'd go against sense just not to look weak.'

Very few of the people involved in the *Tampa* farce are willing to speak, but one member of the crew told Norwegian newspapers after the crisis passed: 'It was a frightening time. We knew that if things turned nasty, we were outnumbered, but we rarely felt threatened. We were more puzzled and angry by the way the Australians were acting, while the refugees went from being weary to angry to weary again. Their travels had taken a lot out of them. But when the SAS came on board, no one knew what would happen next. We were terrified.'

All official requests I made to the Australian Army, Navy, SAS and Government to speak to people involved with the *Tampa* situation went ignored or refused.

Even aside from the *Tampa* situation, Australia has differences from many other countries. The most marked difference is the immigration detention centres around the country or, as Amaz, who had been in one for a couple of months, calls them, 'concentration camps without lethal showers'.

Australia's immigration detention centres include Villawood in Sydney, Maribyrnong in Melbourne, Port Headland, Curtin, Woomera and Perth. Between them, in January 2003, they held around 10,000 people. They are run by Australasian Correctional Management (ACM), a subsidiary of the American private prison firm Wackenhut.

Very few people – including the media – are allowed to see the centres. Secrecy surrounds what goes on inside them, and the contracts between ACM and the Government are regarded as confidential. The running joke is that while the people on the outside want to get in to see what they are like but can't, the people inside want to be almost anywhere else but inside. 'Some refugees have said they would rather go home than stay in them,' claimed Amaz.

Some of those who are allowed in – such as doctors, nurses and lawyers – are reluctant to speak to the media for fear that it may jeopardise their future access to the detainees, or their future contracts with either the Department of Immigration and Multicultural Affairs (DIMA) or ACM.

Campaigners have been begging for years for change, but the Government's attitude seems only to harden over time. A joint parliamentary committee called for improvements to the centres in mid-2001, after having access to detainees directly in six centres without the presence of immigration officials or centre management. Their report stated that they were surprised at the presence of high fences, double gates, razor and barbed wire and shocked at the tales of unsatisfactory medical treatment and limited educational facilities for children.

One member of the group, Colin Hollis, said he had completely changed his opinions after being part of the committee: 'I went from being somewhat of a hard-liner with regard to people who come here to changing my views quite significantly. No one can visit these centres without being profoundly moved – nothing prepares you for the visible impact and I can well understand what leads people to take extreme action.'

Another member, Roger Price, said: 'Australia's detention policy is harsh, ruthlessly implemented and it brings no credit to Australia.' But then-Immigration Minister Philip

Ruddock dismissed their concerns, claiming the committee members were naïve, lacking life experience and were being emotional.

The Government has attacked everyone in its attempts to look better, including the world-renowned *Medical Journal of Australia*, which published a report of the conditions and suffering of people in the camps. Mr Ruddock and his non-medical team wasted no time in attacking the integrity of the report, but all they succeeded in doing was humiliating themselves.

The Australian Government has argued not only with its own politicians and medical experts but also with the United Nations. A UN Working Group on Arbitrary Detention spent weeks in Australia, looking at the camps to assess if they were in breach of the UN's international covenant on civil and political rights. Working group chairman Justice Louis Joinet said the system and its appeal process gave detainees a feeling of 'living in limbo', and that conditions in the Woomera camp were 'dramatic'. A number of issues were raised, including worries over legal obstacles to the reunion of families and concern over an absence of 'points of reference' on how applications for protection visas were progressing. The group pointed out that the system appeared to be 'painfully slow', and it questioned the legality and ethics of using private security firms to run detention camps. There was also concern over musters and headcounts taking place up to four times a day.

Ruddock said the concerns of the UN group were 'news to him'. The official line from the Government is that there are a lot of facilities for immigrants at the centres, including VCRs, DVDs, pay TV, Nintendos and portable hi-fi systems. There are also gymnasium and sporting facilities, pool and snooker tables, and courses in yoga, aerobics and many other things to keep people occupied.

There must also be classes in rioting because there has been damage amounting to around A$20 million done to the centres over the last few years. Questions that come to mind include: Why would you riot in a place that has better facilities and amenities than the average home has? Is life so good that the only fun comes from destruction? The truth of the matter is that, once again, there is duplicity going on. Some centres do not have any of the facilities described and in others they are kept away from the refugees and used by the staff.

One woman who has visited the centres, Naleya Everson, reported that they are nothing like their official description. She said: 'Hearing what these people are meant to have had is quite sick when you know the conditions these people are living in. You know that they're in compounds where they can only see the sky. You know they're being watched by video cameras 24 hours a day. The kind of condition which you expect in maximum-security prisons.'

A nurse who has worked in the centres has also described what she saw. Again, it sounds little like the official line. 'I worked in Woomera for a couple of months. To be honest, it was more like a human zoo than anything else. When you offered them medical treatment, they asked why they were being kept in these conditions. That is if they could speak English. Many couldn't and there were few – if any – translators made available.

'But the DIMA people didn't seem to care about them. They almost grudged being there, having to look after them. Some people didn't even know their basic rights and entitlement and no one from DIMA was informing them.

DIMA people didn't have much time for us either, as they viewed us as being on the side of the refugees. There was very much an "us and them" mentality, with DIMA, ACM and others thinking everyone who criticised them or offered to do things differently was out to get them. Very paranoid.

'The rumours that came out about people or guards sleeping with immigrant women seems to be just scare-mongering, but one thing that is a fact is that the guards could be cruel, taunting the poor people or cruelly teasing them, making them ask over and over again for basics like soap or tampons or shampoo.

'It sounds like a prison, but it wasn't – because there actually was a prison part to the compound and they would throw people in there for anything, even just talking back to guards. I can't say if the guards beat people there, but a lot of people did come back with injuries and marks that they didn't have on going in, and they wouldn't discuss it.

'People who had come from other camps said Woomera was even worse than the others. I don't think there is actually anything better in them, so it's a frightening thought as to how bad the whole system is. It's no wonder there have been riots. Most people wouldn't allow pets to be treated the way these immigrants are and the authorities know this. That's why there are media bans.'

Even more concerns were raised in 2003 when inspectors from the Department of Employment and Workplace Relations published a damning report into the state of the camps. An investigation into Port Hedland revealed there was deadly asbestos in the buildings, fire extinguishers had been removed from accommodation blocks, fire hoses were used to water gardens and there was a lack of staff training. Even more worrying was the revelation that the local fire brigade would not answer a call to the accommodation zone. This investigation took place after ACM staff went on strike over conditions at the camp. The irony seemed to be lost on them that they were not the worst off in the place and those who were had no ability to strike.

All the inmates have left to do is riot. Riots have been taking part on a regular basis and the media has heard of some of them. But the Government does not mind reports of riots getting out because it works in their favour, showing 'how refugees behave'.

The situation looks unlikely to change in the near future. More worrying still, is a question posed by Australia's Refugee Action Committee: 'It is generally agreed that while conditions are similar in all the centres, they are at their worst in the isolated centres like Woomera, because what happens there is not so easily discovered. Therefore it is worth asking the question – if things are bad in the mainland camps, what are they like on Nauru and the other offshore facilities?'

Australia may be one of the earliest lands to deal with immigration on a large scale. And it may be one of the last to find humane and civil ways to deal with the situation.

CONCLUSION

BARRIERS OF LAND OR BARRIERS OF THE MIND? THE 'PROBLEM' OF IMMIGRATION

'Bloody immigrants, stealing our jobs!'; 'Rapist was illegal alien'; 'Prostitute arrested in London was Russian sex slave'; 'Got some workers on the cheap – illegal immigrants, so I can pay them next to nothing and still get away with it.'

Politicians and the media work on what they believe the public want to hear. At the same time, what they say informs members of the population and helps shape their opinions. Many politicians, newspapers and 'people in the street' talk about 'the problem of immigration' and use varying levels of language to discuss illegal refugees entering their country. But what exactly do they define as the problem? Is it the numbers of would-be immigrants? The cost to the receiving country? Or the loss of national identity? Is it a fear of terrorism? Or the illegality of their methods of entry? And when we have defined what the problem is – is there anything we can do about it?

Obviously the more immigrants there are the higher their welfare costs will be, and it is when numbers start to notice-ably rise that many local people start to moan about how the immigrants and asylum seekers are taking their jobs and homes and so on. In Sighthill, Scotland, there were a number of accusations pointed towards the large community of asylum seekers, with people claiming they were stealing homes that Scottish homeless people could have had. There were also tales – exaggerated but sadly based on fact – of some asylum seekers selling off many of the goods their flats had been fitted out with by the local council. There have also been tales in the UK of homeless people ganging up on asylum seekers who have 'stolen our spots', as one homeless man put it. In return some of the seekers have been ganging up on the homeless that they think are after them. The picture of two of society's most needy groups going after each other would be hysterical if it was not so tragic.

It is claimed that immigration is expensive to the receiving country. In fact it is necessary for many Western developed countries because the immigrants both fill vital highly skilled positions and also do the jobs no one else wants to do.

For example, a report for the Labour Market Center Studies at Northeastern University in America shows recent US immigrants were of critical importance to the nation's economic growth in the 1990s, accounting for half the new wage earners who joined the labour force in that period. Looking specifically at men, eight out of ten new male workers entering the workforce in that decade were newly arrived immigrants. Andrew Sum, director of the Labour Market Center, said: 'The American economy absolutely needs immigrants. I realise some workers have been hurt by this, and some people get very angry when I say this, but our economy has become more dependent on immigrant labour than at any time in the last 100 years.'

And this is true not only in America. We saw in chapter 6 that immigrants contribute £2.4 billion annually to the UK economy. Jean-Pierre Chevenement, the former

French Interior Minister, said in 2002 that Europe will need 50 million to 75 million immigrants during the next 50 years to fill jobs. In Italy there were eight workers to every pensioner in the 1950s and there are fewer than four today. Without immigration, that number will dwindle to 1.5 by 2050. In Spain, where the indigenous population is also declining, a migrant army of North Africans does much of the orange- and grape-picking, while Poles and Romanians are much in evidence on Madrid building sites.

'We need immigration,' declared German Chancellor Gerhard Schroeder, who announced plans in 2000 to allow 20,000 non-German computer staff to settle. Germany will need 3 million immigrants a year to maintain the current ratio of workers to pensioners.

Right-wing parties, such as those of Jorg Haider in Austria, Pia Kjaersgaard in Denmark and Filip Dewinter in Belgium, campaign against immigration by playing on fears of a loss of national identity. In democratic societies we have a duty to listen to these groups and debate the points with them. The legacy of colonialism has taught us that the incoming population can all but wipe out an indigenous people and culture, but today's immigration – where migrants are fleeing poverty, or worse – is not on such a massive or aggressive scale. No country has ever had a static population, and each new influx of migrants has added to the richness of that land's culture.

Is the problem the fear of terrorism after the events of 11 September 2001? After 2001 a new and unique 'us and them' mentality became apparent in the West, often starting with the phrase, 'I'm no racist but . . .'. People refused to fly with others who looked as if they came from the Middle East. Mobs attacked 'non-white'-looking people in the streets. Some people – who cannot admit to themselves that they may be racist – have used 11 September to allow themselves subconsciously to pick on those who think differently from them.

But people should always and everywhere have the right to travel to a safer area if they are being persecuted. That is a humane right that no society calling itself civilised can ignore. A handful of potential terrorists is not reason enough for immigration to be viewed as a problem.

So is the 'problem of immigration' that many people act illegally to traffic others? While we have seen that the smugglers see themselves as providing a service, we can also see that the unregulated activity of illegal people trafficking is dangerous and even life threatening. The immigrants are often desperate and vulnerable and as a result are open to abuse.

It seems, to borrow a phrase from former UK immigration minister Barbara Roche, that it is a lack of 'immigration management' that is the problem – not the immigration itself. For instance, in countries such as the UK where asylum seekers are not allowed to work, it is understandable that locals will feel uncomfortable when large numbers of young men with nothing to do suddenly appear. It doesn't mean those young men are any the less deserving of a place in our society.

Some governments react in panic to the general population's various concerns. Early in 2003, Tony Blair threatened to reject the Human Rights Treaty, which obliges Britain to shelter asylum seekers and refugees. He warned that the British Government might re-examine its obligations under the 1951 European Convention on Human Rights. He was specifically referring to Article 3 of the convention, which bans Britain from returning an asylum seeker to a country where their life might be endangered.

But it is not possible to amend the treaty or opt out from any of its provisions, since in 2000 the Labour Government incorporated it into British law under the Human Rights Act. Thus the only way Britain could legally avoid its obligations would be first to repeal its own Human Rights Act; second, to withdraw from the convention completely; third, to enact legislation allowing the UK to exclude undesirables; and fourth, to reapply for membership of the convention, while making clear its reservations about Article 3 and adding a new clause allowing Britain to deport people 'in the interests of national security'.

However, other plans being introduced to the UK under the Nationality, Immigration and Asylum Act 2002 include the removal of the automatic right to benefits for asylum seekers and having British immigration officers in ports across France – and in other countries by agreement in the future – to stop people entering the UK illegally.

But could we really stop illegal immigration, if we wanted to? In Australia, politicians believe they are showing the rest of the world how to deal with the problem and point to the fact that the amount of people applying to come to Australia has halved in the last year. While the figures for illegal immigrants may be entirely different, it is fair to suggest that Australia's harsh policies seem to be working. Geography helps as much as hardheaded policies. But the tide often turns, and the people of Australia should hope that they never face a large disaster or war that forces them to leave, because then they may get a taste of policies similar to those carried out by their government in their name.

Immigration group Project USA believes that there has to be a stop to all immigration – on a temporary basis. A spokesperson said: 'Project USA believes that the United States must reduce legal immigration levels to levels that will enable population stabilisation. This could be accomplished tomorrow by a simple act of Congress. Project USA believes the horrors, violence and chaos that today exists on US borders must be ended. The only way to accomplish this, in our opinion, is to secure the borders so that illegal immigration is not attempted. We believe the best institution for defending US borders is the US military. There should be a moratorium on immigration instituted while our health care and educational systems are fixed, and the Immigration and Naturalization Service is restructured.'

These 'solutions' may address the symptoms of illegal immigration, but they do not address the cause – which is that migration stems from the very real needs of people who are persecuted, impoverished and often homeless to find somewhere safe to live.

Let us, for a moment, be very honest about ourselves. Very few people in Western society stay in the house they were born in. Why? Because better opportunities arise – through education, jobs, income, marriage, pace of life. People move because they think things will be better in the new place, regardless of that new place being two streets or two continents away. The only difficulty we tend to see with this is the frustratingly bureaucratic immigration laws. Yet when we talk about people we do not know moving country, it is suddenly a problem. Perhaps the sad truth is that there is very little that can change while we have this double standard.

Perhaps governments everywhere will realise one day that all people should be treated fairly and given the opportunity to earn a decent wage. Then – and only then – will people think twice about ripping themselves away from their families. There is an old saying that a revolutionary is a person without food, without a roof over their head and a warm fire, and unable to look after their children and loved ones. It is true, most people will live contentedly if they can live like this – there is a lot to be said for having a sense of belonging and community. Sadly, for so many just now, belonging to the wrong community is half their problem, and that is why they move.

I believe the 'problem' of immigration is in ourselves; in our attitudes. By looking at it as a difficulty and not an opportunity, we reveal our own prejudices. Once we can conquer them, everyone can act as global citizens. After all, we are all one people on one big planet.

BIBLIOGRAPHY

American science and engineering' <www.as-e.com>

American Visas <www.americanvisas.com>

Applebaum, A (1995) 'Low-paid jobs we wouldn't touch with a bargepole', *Daily Telegraph*, p 20, 28 February

BBC News <www.bbc.com/news>

Binyon, M (1993) '"Blood right" basis of German citizenship laws under attack', *The Times*, p 10, 15 February

Bird, L (2000) 'Europe's new boat people', *The Times*, weekend supplement p 29, 15 July

Border Action Network team (2000) 'Hate or Heroism: Vigilantes on the Arizona–Mexico Border', <www.borderaction.org>, December

Borjas, G J (1996) 'The new economics of immigration', *The Atlantic*

Brown, L (2000) *Sex Slaves: The Trafficking of Women in Asia*, Virago Press, London

Carroll, S (2003) 'Mohamed Al Fayed's tears as he quits UK', *Mirror*, 2 May

Clancey, P (1999) 'Crackdown on migrant smugglers', *Sun*, p 1, 21 June

CNN <www.CNN.com>

Coalition Against Trafficking in Women <www.catwinternational.orgwww.catwinternational.org>

'Common dreams' <www.commondreams.org>

Connelly, M and Kennedy, P (1994) 'Must it be the rest against the West?', *The Atlantic*, December

Cornwell, R (1995) 'US gets tougher on illegal migrants', *Independent*, p 11, 29 December

Digital Freedom Network
<http://dfn.org/voices/india/slavery.htm>

Eftimiades, N (1998), *Chinese Intelligence Operations*, Newcomb, Virginia, USA

Evans-Pritchard, A (1995) 'Uncle Sam's open door threatens to disunite the States', *Sunday Telegraph*, p 26, 2 April

Federation for American Immigration Reform (FAIR)
<www.fairus.org>

Free the Slaves <www.freetheslaves.net>

Guttenplan, D (2000) 'Right little, tight little island', *Guardian*, p 1, 22 July

Illegal Immigration Australia Website
<http://www.sjc.uq.edu.au/projects/migration>

'Immigration and the public trust' (2000) *Daily Mail* editorial, p 10, 12 September

International Organization for Migration <www.iom.int>

Kaletsky, A (2000) 'America's open house for cheap labour', *The Times*, p 22, 11 May

Kaplan, R D (1998) 'Travel into America's future', *The Atlantic*, July

Langewiesche, W (1992) 'The Border', *The Atlantic*, May

Lowry, S (1994) 'French get tough on illegal immigrants', *Daily Telegraph*, p 14, 7 January

Migration Watch UK <www.migrationwatchuk.org>

Nash, E (2000) 'Spain's immigrant farm workers go hungry in battle over basic rights', *Independent*, p 17, 30 September

Pia, S (2001) 'The shame of "Bella Scozia"', *The Scotsman*, p 2, 9 June

Ryan, N (2003) *Homeland*, Mainstream, Edinburgh

Sacco, J (2000) *Safe Area Gorazde*, Fantagraphics Books, Seattle

'Spain expels its aliens' (2001) *Guardian* editorial, p 10, 26 January

Stelzer, I M (2000) 'Immigration in the new economy',
<www.thepublicinterest.com/archives/2000fall/
article1.html>

'Testimony of Anita Sharma Bhattarai'
<http://www.house.gov/international_relations/hr/
bhattraf.htm>

Tierney, M and Gregory, S (2002) *Forget You Had a Daughter*,
Vision Paperbacks, London

United Nations Office on Drugs and Crime
<http://www.odccp.org/odccp/trafficking_human_beings
html?id=11705>

US Department of State
<http://usinfo.state.gov/topical/global/traffic>

Wheatcroft, G (2000) 'Give us your huddled masses: Far from
being a burden, refugees and asylum seekers could be our
economic salvation', *Observer*, p 30, 2 April

Williams, P ed (1999) *Illegal Immigration and Commercial Sex:
The New Slave Trade*, Frank Cass, London

ABOUT THE AUTHOR

Scottish-born Craig McGill is an experienced journalist with articles in many newspapers, magazines and Internet sites, including *Time*, the *Guardian*, the *Sun*, the *Daily Express*, the *Mirror* and the *Scotsman*. He is the author of *Football Inc.* and *Do No Harm?*, both published by Vision Paperbacks, and of *Hotrods* and *Know the Provo* (forthcoming). He can be reached through mcgill@globalfrequency.org or his website www.craigmcgill.com. For details of his upcoming work, send an email to: cluttereddesk-subscribe@yahoogroups.com.